WANDERING IN THE WILDERNESS

ROBERT BENNE

Wandering In The Wilderness

Christians and the New Culture

PHILADELPHIA Fortress Press

The quotation on p. 51 is from Nikos Kazantzakis, *Report to Greco* (New York: Simon & Schuster, Inc., pp. 291-292). It is reprinted here with the kind permission of the publisher.

Library of Congress Catalog Card Number 72-80401

ISBN 0-8006-0117-3

3225X72   Printed in U.S.A.   1-117

TABLE OF CONTENTS

PREFACE

These reflections on the church and the cultural revolution in American society are aimed at those, both specialists and non-specialists, who are interested in the relationship between Christianity and its social and cultural environment. "Christianity" in this instance means both the Christian faith as a system of religious symbols and the Christian faith as manifested in concrete institutions. Instead of dealing with the effect of the environment on Christianity, this book concentrates on the various effects the church can have on its environment. These include the breadth and depth of meaning that religious symbols can bring to a society that is trying to understand itself, as well as the more direct effects an institution can have on the social and cultural dynamics of a society.

In attempting to bridge many disciplines the book risks losing the sophistication and refinement of more specialized studies. We want to see the "whole forest," and not simply scrutinize several of the individual trees.

Three main strands are synthesized in the following pages: 1) economic, political, social, and cultural analyses that are current in contemporary American writing; 2) theological input that includes the resources of several of the major theologians of our time, the reflections of my colleagues on the faculty of the Lutheran School of Theology at

Chicago, and participation in a theologically alert local congregation that has been stimulated by the Ecumenical Institute of Chicago; and 3) experiments in theological education and parish renewal that have made use of some of the major impulses toward cultural renewal that flow through the American scene.

I owe special acknowledgment to Professors Philip Hefner and William Lesher for their intellectual contributions as well as their cooperation in projects in parish renewal and theological education that have stimulated many of the ideas in the following chapters. Further thanks are in order to the Lutheran School of Theology at Chicago and the American Association of Theological Schools for enabling me to have the free time to put these thoughts on paper, to my wife for encouragement and for help in some of the more unpleasant tasks of preparing a manuscript for publication, and to my three children who have gleefully provided enough disturbance in the environment to push me as a matter of necessity toward the kind of concentration and discipline one needs to write a book.

March 1972   *R.B.*

INTRODUCTION

They set out from Elim, and all the congregation of the people of Israel came to the wilderness of Sin, which is between Elim and Sinai, on the fifteenth day of the second month after they had departed from the land of Egypt. And the whole congregation of the people of Israel murmured against Moses and Aaron in the wilderness, and said to them, 'Would that we had died by the hand of the Lord in the land of Egypt, when we sat by the fleshpots and ate bread to the full; for you have brought us out into this wilderness to kill this whole assembly with hunger.'   Exodus 16:1-3

As this passage indicates, life for the children of Israel seemed to proceed as it often seems to proceed for us, with exodus from bondage leading only into the wilderness. The Israelites' bondage in Egypt had at least been secure: though enslaved, they ate; though controlled, their lives were settled and predictable. Then, through his servant Moses, the Lord put an end to all that and ordered his people out of Egypt. In the beginning, this exodus was doubtless cause for great rejoicing: they were free, and new and greater expectations were open to them. Not even the pain of leaving familiar things behind could have tempered this exhilaration. Gradually, however, as they entered deeper into the wilderness and the days of their wandering seemed ever to increase, they began to lose heart, until finally they rose up and shouted at Moses, "Why did you bring us here? So we could die in the wilderness? We were better off in Egypt! Take us back! Take

1

us back!" Their experience in the wilderness had turned out to be a painful search for identity, fidelity, and purpose.

Both America and the American church have undergone similar experiences. We too have moved through cycles of bondage, exodus, and wilderness. The 1950's, for example, can certainly be looked upon as a period of secure bondage. While fatherly Ike presided over national affairs, settling things down after the turmoil of World War II and Korea, religion took firm hold as one of the social amenities of the American imagination. In 1955 more than half of the American people regularly attended church on Sundays. It was the age of the "package plan" for American missions — a regional staff member of the national church would buy land, erect a building, name it, furnish it, call in a pastor and a professional stewardship expert, and one bright Sunday morning a church would open its doors with every expectation that people would flock to it.

But the Lord would not abandon us to such false security. He pushed us out of it, and the 1960's became our exodus. We experienced a decade that was both dynamic and traumatic, promising and terrifying. Everything became "unstuck." The smoldering racial problem became the civil rights movement and then the black power movement. Institutions expanded and experimented. For the first time in decades, radical politics of both left and right became live options, especially for the young. The war in Vietnam escalated, providing fuel for both the economy and the peace movement. Culturally, what with rock, drugs, underground films, and experimental lifestyles, there was a veritable explosion.

And the church was not unaffected by all this change. Under the leadership of such men as Eugene Carson Blake and James Pike, it involved itself in all kinds of experiments in mission and ministry. In fact, the church during the sixties was perhaps best characterized by its idealism concerning the inner city. Many younger clergymen felt impelled to identify with the poor and the black, and the names of James Groppi, Martin Luther King, and Harvey Cox hit the headlines repeatedly.

If the sixties were our exodus from the secure bondage of the fifties, then the seventies have turned out to be our wilderness experience. Times have changed again, and we find ourselves in a new situation. The scene is the burned out, quiet wilderness where people are asking each other, "Who are we? Where are we going? Did the Lord bring us here to die in aimless wandering?" Our racial policy has become one of benign neglect. The government is pulling back, trying to consolidate whatever gains were made during our time of fermentation. The present administration is engaged in domestic pacification and in winding-down our over-commitments abroad. It is perhaps significant to remember that Richard Nixon was vice-president during the fifties.

The country is, in short, tightening its belt, quieting down, and drawing back. The chic radicals of the sixties have become the mystics of the seventies. Authentic radicals are fewer and angrier—witness the Weathermen and the Berrigans.

As John Lennon of the Beatles put it:

> The dream is over. I'm not just talking about the Beatles, I'm talking about the whole generation, the revolutionary image and the long hair. It's time to own up. It's over and we have to get down to so-called reality.

The church also is being ground into so-called reality. The seventies are proving a new ball game for the church. They constitute our wilderness. Who are we *really*? Where are we going *really*? Are we going to die out here?

The signs of wilderness are all about us. Experimentation throughout the church has been sharply curtailed. The activist, external thrust has become a quieter, introspective quest for identity and integrity. The Groppis, Kings, and Coxes have not been replaced on the front pages of America. Instead, the leadership of the churches has shifted from liberal to moderate or conservative, and the idealism about the inner city has changed to fear and apathy. Seminarians and church bodies are looking elsewhere for action. The social commitments of the church are fewer and made only with tried and trusted partners. The church of the seventies is searching for a new identity in a new situation, fearful that both may be more than it can handle.

But even in the wilderness the Lord's gifts, as well as his chastisements, are evident. The new situation into which we have been pushed by that holy power offers new possibilities as well as new limitations. We can say Amen! to the past. Let us not apologize for the placid fifties or the soaring sixties. They were necessary. They were God's gifts also, for they have brought us to the present moment. We can now decide about the future, a new future. As the children of Israel found out that a new and different people emerged from the wilderness, so also a new and different society and church will emerge in the seventies, and it is clear that we must forge both within our *new* limits and possibilities. We cannot go back to the fifties or sixties. We "can't go home again."

But first, what is the church's new limitation? What has the Lord taken away? He has taken away many of the cultural props that once supported the church and its religion. After the unruly religion of the sixties, American culture is no longer reinforcing and supporting organized religion as it once did. The "package plan" for missions is gone. The active church of the sixties offended and irritated. Funds have now been cut off. Old John Birch left the church in the lurch! Our society no longer finds the churches so useful. Thus, we will increasingly be trimmed of our surplus. Hard times for the church are already here. Seminarians are having difficulty getting a job in an ordinary church, let alone an experimental ministry. Church agencies have cut their programs and financial support drastically. Staff vacancies in most of the agencies of the church are not being filled. All this means real deaths within the church, not only for people but for congregations and worthy programs. The congregation to which I belong tries to survive with no paid personnel. The church of the seventies will be a trimmer and slimmer church.

The coming years offer new possibilities. The grinding of reality—of the Lord himself—is forcing us to clean the rust off the word of God whose bearers we are. And that rough grinding opens the way to several new possibilities.

First, the grinding of the Lord is cleansing the rust of the conservative culture religion of the fifties, which had made God into a "livin' doll" benignly smiling on all that America did. The God of cheap grace, requiring little or no repentance, is gone with the winds of change, and few perceptive Christians now identify Uncle Sam's will in the world with the will of the Almighty. Indeed, many of those who believed that doctrine in one fashion or another have been lopped off by the unruly religion of the sixties.

Secondly, the grinding of the Lord is also cleansing the rust of the naively optimistic culture religion of the sixties in which each new secular movement was hailed as God's new messiah. Secular movements can no longer be mistaken for the mission of the church. It is clear that the church is not essentially a community organization, or a counselling center, or an oasis for small group work, or a seedbed and channel of New Left action. The church of the seventies may utilize and lead to such programs, but must not be grounded in them. Its real mission is unique, and those who do not see that will be increasingly disenchanted with the church of the seventies.

We have been pushed by the Lord of history himself from our secure bondage through an exodus to our own wilderness in which we must find our own unique role before God in this time and place. This is our greatest possibility. After passing through the chastening fires of the Lord we may be able to appropriate anew the word of God for our mission in the world.

Thus, the argument of this book is that the seventies are presenting a decidedly new situation to both church and society. Social fermentation will shift from political and economic to cultural movements that will in turn have later political and economic effects. In these incipient cultural movements the church has an important stake and a significant role. The book has three objectives: an interpretation of the present social and cultural situation; an analysis of new cultural emergents; and proposals for the church's role in relation to them.

First, however, several general definitions are in order. The main definition, and the most difficult, is that of "culture." In the following discussion "culture" refers to the corporate and individual inner consciousness—ideals, values, orientations, perspectives—that lead to a particular style of life. This inner consciousness is of course related to the external world of society; it has been informed and conditioned by the human social world about it. But it is not a carbon copy of external sociality. Indeed, the inner consciousness of each individual can and does influence the external social world in sometimes unpredictable ways by emerging in a lifestyle that interacts with the world. Likewise, external political and economic changes affect style of life and inner consciousness, but again not entirely and sometimes not even very powerfully—witness the persistence of cultural tradition in countries like Czechoslovakia and Poland where political regimes have tried to obliterate individual lifestyles.

Although culture is conditioned by politics and economics, it nevertheless transcends them. And though it cannot be "manufactured" in any simple sense of the word, cultural generation can be encouraged in some measure independently of politics and economics.

Culture and the lifestyle that emerges from it are related to the deepest elements of humanness that all men share. In an obviously over-simplified manner, we would argue that all cultures and their lifestyles address two poles in these deepest elements of humanness. Some cultures and their attendant lifestyles respond to these poles better than others, but all address them in some way. These poles are the *being* pole and the *responsibility* pole.

The being pole can be symbolically expressed by the image of a cup being filled. The cup represents the deepest needs, longings, and aspirations, all the human drives toward self-fulfillment. The liquid being poured in represents the activities of a lifestyle that contribute to the fulfillment of the needs of being. Sometimes the cup is filled by accepting the gifts of others. The need to be loved, for instance, is met by others loving a person and thereby filling his cup. On the other hand, the cup of being can be filled by one's own activities, and the need to love can be met by actively expressing one's affections for another. The need for play, for significant work, and for religious expression are both met and expressed by lifestyle actions that fill the cup of being. These actions are driven by *eros*, the human drive toward self-realization, and all adequate lifestyles address themselves in some way to being. Humans must have something in their cup of being just to survive, but to bear responsibility, which is the second pole of any lifestyle, a more generous amount is needed.

The responsibility pole can be captured in the picture of a cup being poured out. The cup with its measure of being is poured out for others. The responsibility pole of a lifestyle refers to all those activities in which a person spills out his being on behalf of others. In that process he attempts to fill the cups of others, holding forth for them the possibilities of their fulfillment. The examples of such activities are myriad: a man pouring out his energies in his vocation, a mother cleaning a house for her family, a person giving time and energy to a voluntary organization or visiting the sick, and so on. Many responsible roles are not face-to-face activities, and it is easy to lose the sense of pouring oneself out for others in a bureaucratized society, but the image of the cup being poured out is an accurate one. Moreover, if the being pole is driven by *eros*, the responsibility pole is related to *agape*, i.e., love that overflows to others.

An adequate lifestyle deals with both these poles. Its activities fill the cup of being and also find outlets for responsibility. Both poles respond to and express basic humanness. Culture—the inner consciousness of groups and persons—leads to a lifestyle that includes both being and responsibility. Adequate cultures and lifestyles respond with power to the needs of being and the calls of responsibility that lie at the depth of our humanity.

One important final observation needs to be made. Culture is carried and communicated by stories and myths. Such a story or myth includes evocative symbols that organize values, orientations, and perspectives. It thus expresses and stimulates an inner consciousness that leads to a particular kind of lifestyle that responds in greater or lesser degree to the needs of being and the call of responsibility. The Christian story, among others, has been a formative story in western civilization. With its symbols of God, Jesus Christ, the Holy Spirit, and the church, it has evoked lifestyles of great power and variety. Other stories, with their attendant symbols, are also present and active in the modern world.

The Democratic National Convention of 1968 was a traumatic event in more ways than one. Besides the provocations, riots, and counter-riots of that hectic week, the Convention signaled the defeat, at least in terms of that political moment, of the McCarthy movement, which was really a coalition of youth and the left wing of the liberal Democrats. The Yippies and radicals, though present and vociferous, were already so disillusioned with formal politics in America that they met the convention more with sheer protest and ridicule than with persuasive tactics. In the midst of the eruption, it was repeatedly charged that the convention was not representative, i.e., that the real majority of the Democratic Party was not represented. But as the dust cleared, the truth became apparent: some relatively small groups were indeed not represented, but the majority of the Democrats was. The sentiments of the major groups that make up the Democratic party were communicated and effected. Although the national television networks pitched Mayor Daley of Chicago in an unfavorable light, the polls soon made it clear that his actions inside and outside the convention hall were condoned and even applauded by most Americans and most Democrats.

Indeed, it appears that instead of being a distortion of economic and political realities in America, the convention was in fact representative of a new distribution of economic

and political power. The break-down of the old liberal coalition grounded primarily in the urban working classes became
evident. The party that once represented the masses of urban
have-nots still represented the same people, though now they
were part of the middle classes and decidedly not in favor of
pronounced economic and political change. The Convention
of 1968 prefigured the start of the seventies; it raised for the
first time the critical question now facing American
society: Can significant economic, political, and social re-
form occur in a society where most persons are affluent?
Where does sufficient impetus for change come from when a
majority of relatively poor persons can no longer be pre-
supposed?

The Economic Sphere
     The old coalition, forged by Franklin D. Roosevelt, was
based on a majority that was in relative need. In a democratic
society that majority could vote into power the party that
expressed its best interests. The economic structure of the
time, though not the political process, conformed to an age-
old precedent. The economic structure was shaped like a
pyramid with the poor majority occupying the lower part of
the pyramid and the rich minority the upper part. Classical
economists argued that such a structure was inevitable and
that the poor masses would be below the subsistence level. A
line representing the level of subsistence could be drawn hori-
zontally midway across the pyramid. Those below the line
would always be engaged in a rough struggle for survival. The
argument was simple but profound. If the conditions of existence improved for the masses, they would have more children and more of their children would survive. That would
increase the labor force and the supply of labor would sur-
pass demand. Wages would fall back to the bare subsistence
level. This argument, however, was based upon the "labor
theory of value" in which only manual labor was assumed to

have productivity. This theory was oblivious to the fantastic productivity lurking in technology—a technology that was later to have such powerful effects on the economic world.

The theory, then, applied to pre-industrial societies and is still generally applicable to most societies in the world, save the Western industrial societies and Japan. The grim pyramid is still powerfully with us. But with the coming of industrial society and its exploding technology, an economic wonder occurred. The economic structure was moved from a pyramidal shape to that of a diamond. The large middle part of the diamond is made up of the middle class majority, which is constantly rising in affluence. Mankind's increasing domination of the conditions of existence by technology has lifted the majority from the floor of life to its dinner table.

All this should be gratefully applauded. As Reinhold Niebuhr has observed, however, the growth of good is always accompanied by the growth of evil. Technological industrial society has also created problems, of which three stand out.

First, there is still an inverted pyramid in the lower part of the diamond that represents twenty to thirty million persons in the economic backwaters of American society. This segment was dramatically pointed out in the early sixties by Michael Harrington in *The Other America*, which became the stimulus for the War on Poverty that stirred much of the nation in that decade. The twenty or thirty million were those who were passed by in the over-arching economic miracle. The aged, those in poorer economic hinterlands, those discriminated against, and those who in one way or another intentionally have dropped out of society make up that small pyramid at the lower extremity of the diamond. As urbanization and automation heighten, moreover, the plight of "the other America" is made more ambiguous. Forced by circumstances to leave rural areas, immigrants find the city complex and threatening amidst its few promises. Automation tends to decrease the number of unskilled jobs while it increases jobs for the educated. Minimum wage laws in some cases seem only to increase automation and decrease the kind of menial jobs that unskilled persons can cope with. Those locked out of society, e.g., the blacks who were for three centuries denied education and adequate jobs, have in significant numbers become mired in a "culture of poverty" that creates internal, cultural obstacles to mobility in addition to external, social discriminations.

During the sixties, while the middle classes were rapidly moving upward and this bottom segment was on the whole relatively static, the expectations of the poor were lifted by the dramatic promises of the War on Poverty and the civil rights and black power movements. The contradiction between expectations and reality sparked both the urban riots and the revolutionary consciousness of some of the economic underclass and their sympathizers. Although significant movement into the middle class by urban blacks was a reality during the last decade, and though expectations have been dampened, this segment of our society is still laced through with bitterness and despair. Technological society has not been a boon to it.

Secondly, in addition to "the other America," there is the near ecological disaster perpetrated by a careless application of technology to the natural environment. The environment has been extensively altered and polluted by industrialization and urbanization, so much so that it has become questionable whether living organisms are any longer at home in such an environment. Technology has been so unheedingly and voraciously applied to the world that there is a great danger of depleting or polluting many of our indispensable resources. For centuries man was dominated by nature. He tried to wrest a living from an often arbitrary mother earth. Sometimes she destroyed him, but he did not have the potential for destroying her. Technological society has changed all that. We can, and we are, destroying our habitat. We are like a laboratory frog who is in a beaker of water that is gradually being heated, not knowing either how hot the environment really is or precisely when it will become lethal.

Thirdly, the great economic wonder of modern times is rendered highly ambiguous in American society by its being joined too closely to the increase in private, rather than public well-being. The dream of the poor man, that of a material paradise, penetrated our culture from the beginning. The waves upon waves of Europe's poor peasant classes insured that America, with all its technological capacity, would become a consumer society. In fact, the ever expanding production and consumption of private comsumer goods has become the driving principle of American society, a principle supported and intensified by the vast, omnipresent advertising apparatus. The great wealth generated by our technological machine is continually ploughed back into proliferating consumer products.

This wedding of technology with private production and consumption has created what Galbraith has called a "social imbalance." As long as a private world of comfort and affluence can be maintained, the public world can be forgotten. Consequently, in American society, the public world is deteriorating rapidly. Our society has tacitly opted for a color television set in every suburban home rather than for adequate schooling for all. It has chosen beautiful private dwellings over beautiful urban centers. It pays its private executives astronomical sums, but is niggardly with its public officials, and so encourages graft and dishonesty. The crises of the central cities, of mass transportation, of job re-training, of health care, of schools, and of government in general are all related to the American conviction, embedded deep in its citizens, that public undertakings are parasitic on the productive apparatus of the private world. Naturally, therefore, the problems of the other America are exacerbated by a poor and deteriorating public sphere.

Given these three ambiguities and several current trends—the depletion caused by the Vietnam war, increasing American investment overseas, and a slowing down of the American economy—it appears less and less likely that these serious problems will be solved primarily on the economic level. The common wisdom that assumed that most of the problems facing us could be solved by an expanding economy seems false. Even granting that our economy will expand rapidly in the near future, the three problem areas alluded to above will not be solved in that way. An expanding economy will not guarantee that the "other America" will gain sufficient benefits, since the middle class will further its own interest in a rising standard of living. The "other America" itself, at least the parts of it mired in a culture of poverty, will find it difficult to grasp opportunity even if it is offered. A healthy economy will not insure better treatment of the environment. In fact, an expanding economy could have just the opposite effect. Finally, a burgeoning economic realm will not guarantee a re-created and adequately funded public sphere. The wealth could continually be poured back into the private realm for even more luxurious living.

What does all this mean? It certainly does not mean that we can do *without* a healthy economy. But it does mean, contrary to the conventional wisdom of the past, that economic growth alone will not suffice. Our society has gained a sort of maturity. The battle for the future in regard to the problems surrounding the economic sphere will be pitched much more in the realm of man's freedom—his whole culture—than before.

In order for the other America to be grappled with creatively, a cultural renewal must take place both in the poor and middle classes, the classes that hold the economic vote. Among those in the "culture of poverty," a transformation of inner consciousness will have to precede economic mobility. What Banfield calls the "lower class," with its orientation or immediate gratification, cannot and will not join society until it becomes "working class" with a modicum of future orientation. This transformation must take place on the cultural level, the level of lifestyle, or opening doors to economic opportunity will not avail. (In order not to be misunderstood, let me emphasize that many of the American poor are not "lower class" in the above-mentioned sense. They are rather "working class" and can make good use of open doors. Nevertheless, the distinction is an important and useful one, one that has to be made if we are to deal with our problems realistically.)

In order for ecological sanity to be maintained, a new consciousness must penetrate both producer and consumer, and through them the government. The conscious orientation to use as little of nature's resources as possible must supplant the general capitalist ethos that encourages us to use as much as possible. Such a change in consciousness transcends the economic realm. It both assumes and implies a change in culture, in lifestyle.

Finally, an increased concern for the public realm—and all that means in terms of taxes, social justice, and a more modest standard of private living—cannot be generated by resorting merely to economic manipulation. Concerning even these serious economic problems, it seems clear that the health of our civilization is becoming more and more dependent upon a more mature and responsible culture. As the natural conditions of man's life have been controlled, and indeed, dominated by man, there is no longer room in the modern world for heedless economic expansion for its own sake. Man must choose, and his choices are based upon the culture he possesses.

The Political Sphere

If the economic realm is plagued by problems that press for a solution on the cultural level, the same can be said for the political realm. One of the major social theories of our time, the theory of mass society (which has been promulgated in various forms), points to the crisis in the political sphere, a crisis that relates not only to political forms and structures but also to the underlying cultural tendencies of the age.

The theory of mass society postulates the erosion of intermediate group structure in modern industrial societies. The intermediate group is one that is small enough and near enough to the individual to allow him to participate in it effectively. He feels that he is involved in the issues that affect his destiny, and this gives him a sense of identity and community. In American society, voluntary organizations have traditionally fulfilled this role. The ethnic club, the Elks or the Lions, the local unit of the ACLU, the NAACP branch, the parish council, the union local, and various other civic associations are all examples of intermediate organizations. Because they provided channels by which the interests of the man in the street could be transmitted to higher levels, they enabled men and women to feel some connection with society at large. Such organizations also experienced social interaction for its own sake, which contributed further to the development of a sense of identity among individuals. These groups have not by any means completely disappeared from our society, but their strength and functions have been eroded. This has been especially true during the last several years, the economic recession having reinforced the tendency toward withdrawal from public activity. Such intermediate groups now face a difficult struggle for survival.

Their decline can be traced to several causes. The first is the geographical and social mobility stimulated by a dynamic industrial society. Geographical mobility simply means that Americans move around so much—one in five moves every year—that many do not stop long enough to get involved deeply and responsibly in intermediate organizations. One of the churches I belonged to ministered to young junior executives and their wives. They lived in high rise apartments, but only for about two or three years. By then, they had families and had moved farther out in the city or into the suburbs. The church had difficulty encouraging consistent involvement because of the minimal time commitment to the area. When it did elicit a commitment, the church knew it had these people for only a short time and it had to operate with that in mind. Social mobility also tends to erode intermediate group life. Individuals change their acquaintances as they move up the social ladder. They tend, accordingly, to use intermediate organizations for status only and refuse to make serious commitments to them.

Mobility alone, however, could not cause the erosion of such structures. After all, mobility also opens up the possibility for participation in more and varied organizations. The second reason for the decline of intermediate organization is more closely bound up with the lifestyle encouraged by our consumption-oriented society. The absorption into the private life of "pleasurable consumption" needs no public involvement. One does not need to participate in civic activity in order to shop at Gimbels or, better yet, to order articles by mail from Sears. This is the lifestyle—the cultural orientation—encouraged by our society in general and by the advertising media in particular.

As commentators like Maurice Stein have noted, we have moved from an "ethics of production" (the so-called Protestant Ethic, in which the measure of a man was his worth, what he produced and saved) to an "ethics of consumption," in which status is determined by the style of consumption, by what one buys and uses. The sales pitch for this lifestyle is not coercive, but it is persuasive and it penetrates a very large segment of our society. This lifestyle, combined with high social mobility, leads to a rootlessness and isolation that is healthy neither for individuals nor society. It deprives individuals of any sense of "belonging" and isolates them from the decisions that affect them, so that they become cynical and apathetic toward public life and redouble their unfulfilling efforts to find satisfaction in consumption. Such persons, so the theory of mass society argues, become highly susceptible to right wing extremist movements, which play on their nostalgia for the largely imaginary "old days" when there was real community and political responsibility.

In recent years two major movements have been mobilized to recreate the intermediate level of political organization. The first was the community organization movement, which began in earnest in the early sixties and continues to struggle for survival today. This was an effort to overcome the rootlessness and isolation from power of local citizens. It began in the poor black ghettoes of urban America, but is now being tried in suburban areas also. It attempts to elicit from large numbers of persons active participation in groups that are not threatening or alien to them. Their leaders then try to transmit the self-interest of the persons they represent to higher levels of decision-making. Many valuable insights into methods of organization have been gained from this movement and it promises to offer more such wisdom in the future.

But the community organization movement itself has found out that it too is dependent upon a prior cultural task. Unless there are persons in the community whose lifestyle permits them to assert themselves in public activity, the movement tends to degenerate into elite organizations. In many areas where community organizations are operating, they are dependent upon churches not only for money but also for persons who are "turned on" to political action. Though partially successful, the community organization movement has itself demonstrated that cultural renewal must precede the re-creation of intermediate organization. More-over, this need for cultural transformation will become increasingly acute as community organization moves into suburban areas, where self-interest is not as sharply defined by "gut-level" feelings as in the ghettoes.

The second major effort at resuscitating local political action was the New Left movement. This began as a fairly unified student movement but later splintered into scores of ideologically antagonistic groups. Those groups that are not already defunct have become so extreme and hardened in their ideology and rhetoric (e.g., the Weathermen and the Maoist factions) that they have become irrelevant to the broader political world. Though angry, they offer no real threat or promise to American society. But the early student political movement was significant in its attempt to renew grass roots democracy, and the very failures of the movement indicate again that cultural transformation is a necessary prerequisite for political renewal. Not lack of motivation, but unrealistic perspectives precipitated the movement's downfall. Indicative of this lack of realism was the overstatement by the leaders of the corruption of American politics and society. America was judged not by the measure of what actual societies in the past or present had attained, but rather by ideal standards of pristine purity. This, and the New Left's breathless expectation of apocalyptic change created either by the immediate disintegration of a corrupt America or by a revolutionary movement of hazy definition, quickly discouraged the mainstream society from taking the New Left seriously.

The Cultural Sphere

Thus far we have argued that the movement of history itself, especially through the technological revolution, has created a new world with new problems. These problems are spinoffs from economic and political changes but they demand for their amelioration a new consciousness, a new cultural orientation, in man himself. In short, cultural

transformation must precede the needed economic and
political changes. This argument is similar to that advanced
by social philosophers such as Peter Viereck and Victor
Ferkiss. Viereck, for instance, points to a "revolution of the
heart" taking place in Communist countries that transcends
the cold and hardened political realities of the public world.
This revolution, expressed in poetry particularly and creating
a new consciousness among youth, will doubtless have
political effects in the future.

Ferkiss asserts that the technological revolution has altered
the conditions of man's existence in highly ambiguous ways,
offering both threat and promise. But the technological
apparatus needs a new man—technological man—to make sure
that the promises and not the threats emerge in the last part
of the twentieth century. Ferkiss awaits a cultural revolution
also. He admits that the old bourgeois culture is tired and
incompetent, and rules now only by default. Indeed, in his
opinion, bourgeois man is at the helm of a technological
juggernaut and has neither the desire nor the wisdom to steer
it in a humane direction.

Two remarks from other writers also express this belief in
a kind of cultural exhaustion. Arend van Leeuwen says:

> The perlexing thing is that just at the moment when the West may
> be achieving the conditions which make leisure for all practicable, it
> is spiritually dessicated; whilst the East is so eager to seize hold of
> our technics that in the process it loses sight of its own values—
> values of which we all stand in the greatest need.

Michael Harrington reflects in the same vein:

> At precisely that moment in history where for the first time a people
> have the material ability to end poverty, they lack the will to do so.

The problem we face, therefore, is a cultural one. It con-
cerns basic human consciousness, the basic images of self and
world that form the identity and values that make for a

satisfying and responsible life. If it is true that our economic and political problems press for solution on the cultural level and that the strength of the cultural level itself is questioned, then we must look at this cultural crisis from a historical perspective.

Ernst Troeltsch, at the end of his *Social Teachings of the Christian Church*, summarized what he thought was the kernel of the Christian ethos. He found it to be constituted by two foci: an intensive aspect—radical love for the brethren—and an extensive aspect—universal scope. When the Christian ethos is vital, these two aspects are in creative tension. The radical love motif presses for a warm and intimate communal life enhancing all the values of human inter-relations. But this radical love cannot be content with remaining locked within an exclusive community. It must penetrate the whole world because the world is God's and by his love, as expressed through his people, he wills its perme-ation. Thus, the ethos of the early Christian community was inevitably pushed outward into the surrounding world.

With the decline of the Greek and Roman civilizations of antiquity and with its unobtrusive inception in the life, death, and resurrection of Jesus Christ, the Christian ethos gained tremendous momentum and spread like wildfire throughout the Near East, northern Africa, and southern Europe. Its spread was not aided by official imprimatur nor by the approval of the upper classes. Christianity swept through the world with its own contagious power. The first three hundred years of the Christian era was what Paul Tillich called a "theonomous" period. From the very depths of reality, the power of God erupted spontaneously in the lives of Christian people. This forging of the Christian ethos was so powerful and enduring that it provided the underlying cul-tural substratum for at least fifteen hundred years, a period that filled the wells of Christian consciousness from which many different lifestyles were drawn.

Until the fourth century, when the Emperor himself became a Christian, the intensive aspect of the Christian ethos—radical love—had provided the church's main impetus. With the conversion of Constantine, however, the emphasis shifted to the extensive aspect—universal scope—which had, of course, been implicitly operative all along. From 300 to 1500 the Christian ethos had its chance to penetrate all of human life; economics, politics, art, literature, music, and law were all gathered under its umbrella. It provided the glue that not only penetrated these elements of culture but also brought them together into a unified whole. The medieval ages strove toward that elusive goal, a "Christian" civilization. But though some parts of the Middle Ages were indeed "theonomous," like the first three hundred years of the Christian era, other parts can be termed "heteronomous," i.e., Christian practice and lifestyle were coercively applied to persons and the dimensions of common life. The Emperor, after all, had the power to make Christianity *the* religion of the realm. Unfortunately, heteronomy tends to spoil exactly what it is trying to promote. Inevitably, the Christianity of the 14th and 15th centuries became corrupt.

The Reformation in its various forms attempted to reclaim the vital kernel of the Christian religion and, to a goodly extent, it succeeded. The Christian ethos again flowered forth spurred on in part by the Reformation even as, in combination with classical culture, it had also appeared in the achievements of the Rennaissance. In this period, a religious meaning was given to worldly vocation and new resources of individual responsibility and energy were poured into the building of the earth.

Shortly thereafter, the new life brought forth by the Reformation gave birth to the bourgeois revolutions that once and for all took the realms of economics and politics out of the hands of the medieval church and the feudal order. The bourgeois revolutions spawned the industrial societies of the eighteenth and nineteenth centuries, and the "Protestant Ethic," as Max Weber termed the Calvinist cultural perspective, may be said to have helped provide the impetus for them also. This Protestant Ethic continues to survive in Western culture to this day, but as Troeltsch and Weber both agreed, its religious substance began to diminish shortly after the Reformation and was gradually drained out of it altogether, until finally it stood autonomous, characterized chiefly be a preoccupation with gainful employment, an ascetic manner, and a cold rationality. Devoted to productivity and profit, it helped to erect a great industrial and technological superstructure that has changed forever the face of the earth.

As Troeltsch and Weber both argue, however, such a demanding style of life cannot be maintained without strong religious underpinnings. The Protestant Ethic has become in the twentieth century the consumption ethic; though the driving, frugal, and disciplined elements have all but disappeared, the acquisitiveness has remained. Troeltsch and Weber were both pessimistic about the development of Western civilization in this century because they believed that the Protestant Ethic had lost its religious dimension and that what was left lacked the strength, discipline, and humanity to control and humanize the industrial order that even in their day had reached gigantic proportions. They saw developing a bureaucratized industrial superstructure that eventually would move through history under its own momentum and demand homage from a flaccid and placid society. Both concluded their studies with the prediction that Western culture would need to be replenished before modern society could be made conducive to human fulfillment.

From a more secular point of view, Philip Rieff has reached the same conclusion. In his study, *The Triumph of the Therapeutic*, Rieff divides history into categories that resemble those of Troeltsch. He believes that there have been

four basic types of man in human history. The first was
political man, the Greek and Roman ideal, who devoted his
life to the polis as a citizen, living a modest life in private.
With his passing, religious man reigned for at least a thousand
years. Religious man had as his goal the contemplative ideal,
the vision of God. The path to that ideal was an ascetic and
disciplined life. Economic man, though more short-lived than
his forbears, flourished for several centuries right up to the
twentieth century. His commitment was to the marketplace,
in which his goal was the building up of his economic empire,
whether great or small. He, like the Protestant in Weber's
study, was frugal and ascetic in his private life. These three
types all had in common a commitment to something outside
themselves. They had a cause to which they could devote
their lives' energies. They practiced what Rieff calls a
"therapy of commitment." By creatively renouncing their
wishes for immediate pleasure for the sake of a cause greater
than themselves, they sublimated their energies to that cause.
The community in which they lived shared these goals and
rewarded their sublimation accordingly.

Rieff believes, however, that there has been a great cultural
shift in recent years. Economic man has passed away also,
and a new man, psychological man, has taken his place. What
distinguishes psychological man from the earlier types is his
break with the therapy of commitment. His goal is no longer
connected with a cause outside himself. Instead, his aim is to
achieve a pleasureable interchange with his environment. By
carefully counting his satisfactions and dissatisfactions, he
avoids unprofitable, i.e., unpleasureable, commitments. When
involvements become too demanding, he withdraws gracefully from them. He fits hand-in-glove with a consumer-
oriented society, and he is not one who will plunge decisively
into the problems of the new technological society and tame
the autonomous industrial machine. He is neither a great
villain nor a great hero.

We might describe psychological man as a "floater." He surrounds himself with friends and involvements, but his commitments are always partial. He gives a bit of himself to this person and a smidgeon of himself to that cause. In this manner, he spreads himself thinly over the spectrum of his life. He floats over history like a leaf in a stream, making scarcely a ripple as he pursues his goal of pleasureable negotiations with the world. We should not get the idea that the floater is a dishonorable scoundrel. His floating is actually a defense mechanism, either conscious or unconscious, designed to protect himself from painful responsibilities.

Up till now in American history we have been able to move forward on the momentum of inherited lifestyles. But the 1970's have brought us into a new situation. More know-how, more production, more consumption will be to no avail. The imperative has become the renewal of our culture.

American society is the first in history to pose these questions: When a free society can wrest an almost limitless private standard of living from nature, will it be able to *choose* to live according to reasonable needs rather than limitless desires? Will it be able to choose to channel an adequate amount of its energies into the public sphere, into the broader, less fortunate world, and into a higher quality of life?

Other societies have never been confronted with such questions. They either have not had the technological capacity and natural resources to create such affluence or if they have (as Russia does) they have had authoritarian political regimes that have prevented any choice from being made. Will a free society be able to choose a "higher" life for all? Or will it fritter away its potential by mindlessly pursuing increased production and consumption with all its technological might? If the latter is the case, all the problems we have pointed to will increase tenfold. Minority poverty, public poverty, political isolation, rootlessness, autonomous technology, and an exhausted culture will bury us.

If our thesis is correct, and the seventies are to be our wilderness as the sixties were our exodus, then they also embrace, as the original wilderness period did, evidences of hope. The aim of this chapter, accordingly, is to point to some of the manna that is coming our way in the midst of our wilderness. The sources of renewal that we will be examining are not directly political or economic but cultural. Eventually, they will have important political and economic effects, some of which we will try to elaborate. At present, however, these cultural building blocks operate solely at the level of consciousness; they come to us in the form of new attitudes, values, and perspectives that manifest themselves in behavioral changes, i.e., in new lifestyles. The genesis of these building blocks lies in the past, certainly before this new decade began. But though they originated then, they seem now to be increasing in size and strength and making an impact on significant numbers of persons. Indeed, the three that we shall discuss are having such impact that together they may be said to constitute a cultural revolution.

These three impulses are the growth of the youth culture, the small group movement, and the development of task-oriented intentionalism. The first two are characterized somewhat by their labels, but the third deserves a word of explanation. It has to do with the increasing availability and use of self-conscious planning methodologies in corporate and individual life. The methods and disciplines by which groups and individuals are able effectively to project their own intentions into the future are affecting the consciousness and lifestyles of great numbers of persons and institutions.

Several additional comments can be made about all three emergents. It is no accident that they in particular have erupted at this time. Each responds to deep human needs that have been neglected or suppressed in contemporary lifestyles. They are the manna in the wilderness that we need in order to begin the task of cultural rebuilding. They have erupted from the Ground of Being itself, and they present us with the opportunity to create a consciousness and lifestyles more adequate to present and future situations. They create only opportunities, however, not guarantees. Each has its own ambiguities and its own possibilities for use and abuse.

The youth culture is oriented to what we have called the being pole in lifestyle. It is at its heart a religious quest. It asks the questions of basic identity: Who are we? What do we come from? How do we relate ourselves to the reality that threw us into existence? At its best, the youth culture presses toward an appropriation of the mystery of human existence. It stands in wonder before it and celebrates the basic "O.K.-ness" of life. In doing so it fills its cup of being.

The small group movement stands at the juncture of the being and responsibility poles. It is at its heart a quest for interpersonal depth. In the exploration of interpersonal space, the cup of being is filled. Persons are affirmed and intimacy is shared. Persons grow in self- and other-understanding. Moreover, with its emphasis on self-affirmation and the need to be loved, the small group movement carries an additional gift: it opens up possibilities for increased authentic responsibility among persons in face-to-face situations.

What we have called "task-oriented intentionalism" moves over to the responsibility pole in lifestyle. It is interested in .

how the cup of being can be most efficiently poured out, both corporately and individually. How can the images that man conjures up be projected into future reality and systematically realized? How can man *make* history in a self-conscious and comprehensive manner? These questions concerning the problem of man's responsibility for his world and his history are wrestled with by our third cultural impulse.

The Youth Culture

After so many books and perspectives on youth—Roszak, Reich, Earisman, Benson, Winter, Saffen, Erikson, and Keniston are only a few that come to mind—it seems almost ridiculous to talk of "a" or "the" youth culture or even to write about youth. But the amount of attention given to this cultural phenomenon itself indicates that it is something more than the creation of the mass media. With its roots in the Beat Generation of the fifties and the New Left movement of the sixties, the development of the contemporary youth culture is making its impact felt in the broader culture. Except for a few small but vociferous groups, the political strand that flourished in the sixties is almost extinct. (The exception is the pacifist wing of the peace movement, which shares more characteristics of the youth culture and therefore flourishes more than its highly alienated and angry political brethren, such as SDS.) Moreover, the youth culture by no means embraces the majority of American youth—though it is startling to find that certain of its characteristics have penetrated to some of the most unlikely hinterlands of the Western world. (American rock music blaring out of a jukebox in a small Bavarian town continues to surprise me, especially when it is being danced to by long-haired youths in Lee jeans and tie-dyed shirts.)

The youth culture we are talking about includes three basic characteristics. First, it searches for a *non-dominating harmony with reality*—a symbiotic relation, one might say.

Second, it is extremely *expressive*. Finally, it is incorrigibly *experimental*. Let us elaborate these one by one.

In response to the centuries-long movement to dominate and control the natural conditions of existence, the youth culture now is bearing a strong counter-current that aims at living in a more symbiotic harmony with nature. There is a revived naturalism at work, not a scientific naturalism, certainly, but rather a romantic one. Instead of using rational methods of control over nature, there is pre-rational identification with nature. Furthermore, instead of emphasizing the elevation of man over nature, man is seen as part of nature and her children. The concrete manifestations of these attitudes appear in the imitation of American Indian culture, in a preference for organic foods, in ecological sensitivity, and in a rather anti-urban bias. These attitudes extend beyond nature to the human world and result in a strong pacifist tendency among youth. In trying to negate the striving aggressive spirit in man, representatives of the youth culture emphasize instead the natural human impulses and drives; these, they maintain, are self-limiting and satiable. In fact, generally speaking, the "flower child" of the post-Haight-Ashbury type exhibits a winsome naivete about human motivations, especially his own. All these elements fit together and are obvious in two of the most important film portrayals of the youth culture, *Easy Rider* and *Alice's Restaurant.*

This revived naturalism, however, is not characterized solely by a secular dimension. First through drugs and later through Eastern mystical techniques, the youth culture has tried to give it a religious dimension. Its sense of identification with nature has·led it to seek the divine in the immanent natural systems and processes in which all beings participate. To the question "Who are we?," it answers "We are natural creatures who carry within us the wisdom of millions of years of evolution. We can trust our inclinations and feelings and follow them. We participate in a whole interrelated system of life that is also basically good and trustworthy, and certainly wonderful and full of mystery. Our imperative is to adapt to this holistic system with as little disruption of natural patterns as possible." It should be mentioned that some of the latest religious impulses of the youth culture seem to be returning them to explicit Christian symbols, so that now the Jesus-cults are competing with the Eastern religions for new devotees.

If the first characteristic of the youth culture is religious naturalism, its second is its capacity for *expression*, for spontaneous play. The religious moment is a passive one in which underlying reality is appropriated and appreciated. The second moment is active: it is the expression of the internal state of consciousness in song, dress, movies, art, and literature. There are still songs of social and political protest, but several of the major musical creations of the Beatles, the Moody Blues, Baez, and many others seem to fit more into the religious and aesthetic motif. There is also, of course, hard rock, which expresses in sublimated form the more aggressive and violent sentiments of youth. But at any rate, its music is extremely important to American youth and it is, to say the least, powerfully expressive.

The playful elements of the youth culture can be seen in films like the Beatles *Hard Day's Night* or *The Yellow Submarine*. Fashion will never be the same now that youth has reintroduced long hair, bright and fancy men's clothing, bell-bottoms, head-bands, and beads. Unrestrained expressiveness has also erupted in the language, art, and literature produced in the youth culture. Vigorous inventiveness is the rule of the day and very few old forms seem able to bear the energy of the new inventions. This inventive expressiveness must be seen against the background of the parents of these young persons. A generation that experienced the struggle and drabness of the Depression and two wars was naturally more serious, restrained, and frugal. But with growing affluence and cultural tolerance, the youth of today are far from restrained.

Closely related to expressiveness is the third characteristic of the youth culture. It is consistently *experimental*. The new and different must be better than the old, especially if youth has dreamed up the new. We have already mentioned experimentation in music and the arts, but another case in point is the proliferation of communes, in which new sexual and familial relationships are grist for experimentation. The number of urban and rural communes has greatly increased, as have experimental approaches to education, the latter chiefly in the form of counter-universities and free schools. Indeed, "straight" education, with its lectures and exams, has become a virtual impossibility for many of today's youth.

As a professor in a theological seminary and an inveterate visitor to many churches, I am particularly impressed by the extent to which these three characteristics of youth culture have penetrated church life. I find myself writing more and more recommendations for conscientious objector status for seminary students who are pacifists in principle and who no longer will accept the deferred status our country gives to pre-theological students. In an urban area like Chicago, communes with an explicit religious consciousness and discipline are easy to find. The rock cantatas, the folk song liturgies, and the multimedia worship services are all too familiar to detail here. The interest in the "Jesus story" has been renewed not only in the culture but in the church. *Jesus Christ Superstar* is performed in church colleges throughout the land and books of an evangelical nature sell like hot cakes in college and university bookstores.

The spread of the youth culture has been largely due to the mass media, of course. For there have been other historical periods when perhaps these three characteristics have appeared among youth. In fact, Paul Tillich describes the youth movement in the Germany of the 1920's in roughly similar terms. But the movements of the past were always limited to certain classes, especially those who could attend the universities. Such is not the case today. The mass media have made this new consciousness available to all classes of young persons. Though the majority of devotees no doubt come from the middle and upper middle classes, it is also evident that working class youth has been affected as well. A genuine youth subculture has been created by these pervasive influences. It has and will play an increasingly important role as the time between late adolescence and the embarkation into a vocation is lengthened by longer preparation for increasingly sophisticated jobs. The youth subculture will provide a base for identity and values for the "in between" group of persons, and the consciousness developed then will continue as young persons take their places in the adult world.

What will be the long-run economic and political effects of these three characteristics? For one thing, the economy of the country will probably be dampened by a generation less oriented toward conspicuous consumption. Young persons are quite aware that increased consumption pushes us nearer to ecological disaster and so they tend to live more in accordance with basic needs than with superfluous wants. The tendency to live more "naturally," with fewer artificial props, will also narrow the market a bit. In a semihumorous vein, we can already note that the men's barber and woman's undergarment industries have felt the effects of the youth revolution. More seriously, after several generations of striving for a higher and higher standard of living, we seem now to have a generation that is more inclined to lower its standard of living.

There will also be less competitive drive in the generation affected by youth consciousness. Less disciplined energy and aggressiveness logically accompany a group of persons more oriented to expressiveness. This is play in its best sense. The youth culture produces "softer" individuals who are more tolerant and contemplative than their elders. These qualities will have long-term economic and political effects also. The playing down of aggressiveness and its attendant political orientation, pacifism, has already influenced the armed forces of this country. In the long run, there will be fewer persons ready to fight in a war or to strive aggressively in the political sphere, the youth's own revolutionary rhetoric notwithstanding.

Moreover, partly because of the heightened awareness of social problems that it owes to the mass media and partly because of its self-separation from the moorings of the past, there will be more anxiety and uncertainty in the developing generation. Its sharp awareness of social problems is not matched by a like amount of involvement, and its experimentalism tends toward prolonged and frenetic searches for the holy grail. Unfortunately, persons in whom uncertainty is wed to a highly imaginative inventiveness tend to waver drastically between high and generally unrealistic hopes, and darkest despair. The only target for this kind of free-floating anxiety is an abstract "establishment", and it becomes the whipping boy.

In short, we see the youth culture having ambiguous political and economic effects. Its latent political and economic effects (slowing down the economy will be the primary one) are more important than its manifest ones. It will not be known for stimulating the responsibility pole of lifestyle. Rather, its abiding contribution to cultural change will fasten on the being pole. It has broken through a "closed" worldview in which reality was measured and objectified, in which the depth and wonder of experience in the world was leached out by the mentality of domination. This "mentality of domination" was not the product of self-consciously malevolent men. It was much more the by-product of an increasingly successful technological revolution and the failure of cultural institutions to create lifestyles that could keep apace with them.

Those young persons affected by the youth culture are much more open to religious experience than their fathers and grandfathers. After centuries of creeping desacralization of the world, the youth culture has broken through the one-dimensional quality of the modern world. This will make possible a new religious consciousness for the modern world—a major contribution to filling the cup of a heretofore flattened-out existence.

The Small Group Movement

If the youth culture has been elaborated by the young and transmitted through the mass media, the small group movement was begun by musty middle-aged academics and transmitted in its early days through training laboratories. The movement has now disseminated so broadly that one could hardly call it either "middle-aged" or "academic." Indeed, in every major and most minor metropolitan areas training centers with luridly inviting names like "Oasis" or "Encounter" have proliferated. Colleges and universities offer practical seminars in group dynamics; churches have their koinonia groups in which small group methods are used; and businesses send their executives to training sessions at places like Bethel, Maine, so that they can relate more effectively to their cohorts. "Rap-groups," less formal spin-offs of the small group movement, abound in education and protest movements of various sorts, and books like Berne's *Games People Play*, Harris's *I'm OK, You're OK*, and Schutz's *Joy* all closely related to and used by small group approaches, remain on best-seller lists for months. Certainly something of major proportions is happening in all this. Let us examine some of the dynamics of the movement. What is it and why did it develop? What is its basic approach and what are its effects?

The groups we have alluded to above go under many different names—group dynamics, sensitivity groups, encounter groups, growth groups, training groups, and human potential groups, to name a few. All converge in the intent to provide through a trained leader a context and a methodology where persons can break through their "normal" patterns to deeper levels of self-awareness as well as to modes of communicating at greater depth with others both inside and outside the "training group." These groups, operating with relatively normal persons, should be distinguished from therapy groups in which serious emotional and psychological disorders are treated. The groups under discussion rightly assume that through increased self-awareness and deeper levels of communication some of the most satisfying of human potentials are unlocked. When these methodologies operate at their best they really do provide ways in which persons can fill their cups.

Through the group process greater self-acceptance becomes a possibility. Persons can be affirmed and accepted in ways they never before experienced. Moreover, by virtue of this greater self-acceptance they learn how to share their emotions and feelings with others, and they deepen their level of interaction with their fellows. When these things happen, persons experience a strength and fullness they did not feel before, and when they find their cups of being relatively full, they find also that they have enough in them to risk some of it by moving toward deeper relations with others. In reaching out to others, they take the responsibility to confront, give feed-back, affirm, and generally to stick with a person. As we said earlier, in terms of lifestyle the small group movement stands at the juncture of the being and responsibility poles; it enables persons to fill their cups and to learn to fill the cups of others in face-to-face relationships.

The small group movement in its various facets has emerged strongly at this time for several reasons. First, social and geographical mobility have torn persons from the land, from the familiar small town, and most importantly, from the extended family. The sense of familiarity, of closeness, of being at home in the given company of one's human peers has been eroded by the acids of modernity. True enough, new kinds of relationships can be built, but one must choose these and have the courage to follow through on them. Great numbers of mobile middle class individuals have not been able to achieve the familiar human context they experienced in earlier life. Metropolitan areas are teeming with persons who feel lonely and rootless, and who yearn nostalgically for closer ties with others. In addition to mobility, our society has also undergone bureaucratization; individuals work in large companies where roles are carefully and rationally defined. Bureaucracy enhances the values of competitive efficiency rather than those of human warmth and familiarity. Hence, persons who work in large companies and live in mobile communities are good candidates for participation in small groups.

A second reason for the increasing popularity of small groups is the traditional restraint that is a characteristic of Protestant culture. Ascetic Protestantism frowned upon the free expression of emotion in human relations. Emotion was a sign of weakness and therefore forbidden. Recent generations, however, have more readily accepted the notion that expressed emotion in human relations, be it love or anger, is necessary in the process of humanization, and small groups generally appeal to persons who want to learn such expression.

Finally, as Troeltsch so accurately noted, with the gradual weakening of the Christian ethos during the past centuries, the Christian churches have not been generating communities of radical love. They have lost their power to become demonstration models of the "blessed community," which is what they were called to be. The small group movement has attempted to fill this vacuum left by the churches.

We should point out some of the social consequences of this movement. Perhaps the greatest is the pressure it has mounted toward the democratization of institutional life in America. The small group approach is radically democratic, demanding decisions on a consensus basis and eliciting the participation of all in the group process. It is inherently anti-authoritarian. Already enough persons have been through small group training to make an impact upon business, church, and educational institutions. Even the army is feeling this pressure toward democratization. In tandem with the youth culture, the small group movement will increasingly question leadership roles based on ascribed, rather than earned, authority.

A movement with so much potency cannot help but have its dangers, and the small group movement has its share. The greatest is perhaps its tendency to entice persons away from the public sphere. The joys and excitement of exploring intimate space with a methodology that works are alluring. The great social problems facing the nation are not amenable to such a sure methodology and involvement in them is certainly not as directly rewarding. Moreover, temptation to withdraw from public responsibility for the sake of private fulfillment is especially strong for those who are already affluent and are insulated from exposure to social problems.

A second danger is the abuse of the small group methodology by untrained or malicious individuals. Because the small group approach is so popular, many self-proclaimed experts hold training sessions. Participation in groups under such leadership runs the risk of running into problems that are beyond the competence of the leader. In such circumstances, a lot of harm may be done to the participants. This is especially the case when the untrained leader and/or other participants get their kicks out of hard, angry feedback. If there is no "working through" the negative feedback, the group experience can be very destructive to unsuspecting members.

Finally, and not least in importance, the small group methodology may be proclaimed by some as God's new messiah. It then becomes the gimmick that will solve all our problems. The true believers in this movement, both professional and lay, try to make it the center of education, church life, business life, and everyone's personal life. If it is given such status it quickly leads to phoniness—false intimacy, short-term emotional binges, and illusory gains.

The church has been penetrated by the small group approach, just as it has by the youth culture. It first moved into seminary education through the Clinical Pastoral Education programs that have been established in many hospitals across the country. Here students experienced small group training with their peers under professional leadership. They were turned on enough by that to respond with enthusiasm when pastoral care programs introduced group dynamics into the regular curricula of many seminaries and schools of theology. With increased accessibility of training in the broader society, more and more professors and students were exposed to this training. Now the methodology is used in many of the innovative approaches to theological education within the seminaries. Moreover, it is used in disciplines other than pastoral care, for example, systematic theology, social ethics, and religious education. And from the seminaries the approach has gained entrance into parish life in the form of koinonia groups, circles, and retreats.

Its presence in the seminaries and the church has been subject to the same kinds of use and abuse found in society at large. Some of the practitioners forget about social responsibility, others try to use the methodology before they are trained, and still others proclaim it as *the* solution to all that ails the church. By and large, however, the movement has had a beneficial effect on the church and its attendant institutions. Democratization has been introduced where one would scarcely have expected it a few years ago. Churchmen have gained immediate experience of what human affirmation and forgiveness are like, many of them for the first time in their adult lives. Their self-awareness and their capacity for ministering to other persons have both grown. The experience has stimulated a change in consciousness and lifestyle within the church, as it has indeed done in the society at large. It is one of the impulses toward cultural renewal.

Task-Oriented Intentionalism

Both of the renewal impulses already discussed lean toward the being pole of lifestyle. They are concerned primarily with filling the cups of individuals. The religious thrust of the youth culture responds to the deepest needs of humans to live in an ultimately meaningful world. The youth culture is a vehicle of mankind's attempt to appropriate the mystery of the givenness of life. The small group movement has been an attempt to recapture the enriching depths of self-awareness and interpersonal communication. This not only fills the cup of being, it also enables individuals to be more responsible in interpersonal relations. The small group movement in this way pushes toward the responsibility pole.

Our third impulse toward cultural renewal presses far over toward the responsibility pole. Indeed, its main interest focuses on the intentional changing of the structures of human life. It aims for the self-conscious forging of history. This makes it different from both the youth culture and the small group movement. The former tends toward actions of which the aim is only to express a state of inner consciousness, and not to change the world. Change, of course, may be a by-product. As for the small group movement, even in its encouragement of responsibility, it remains in the private sphere. It has public side-effects, but it is not self-consciously directed toward them.

Only what we have called "task-oriented intentionalism" holds this public effect uppermost. It is both a stance toward life and a methodology. Intentionalism as a stance demands the exercise of man's finite freedom. Man is free to thrust his life significantly into history, and it is this that constitutes his greatness. Man does not have to be a victim of circumstances, and the agenda of his life does not have to be determined by the onrushing situation. Modern man in particular experiences himself, both corporately and individually, as an agent in the creation of the future. There are no immutable laws relentlessly grinding out his destiny. Instead, there are powers, forces, and probabilities, all of which he relates to as controller and determiner. Man, now come of age, is the creator of his own history.

As a methodology, task-oriented intentionalism is a systematic way of building comprehensive models to impress upon future reality, of making the necessary decisions to realize the models, and of the organizational development needed to implement those models and decisions. In short, intentionalism is the fullest use of man's planning ability. It is the systematic planning of change.

Both as a stance and as a methodology, intentionalism is being impressed upon our culture by various groups. As a stance it is appearing most powerfully in the black revolution, the women's liberation movement, the community organization approach, and in such church groups as the Ecumenical Institute in Chicago. Concerning the blacks, the women, and the poor, the basic problem is not in the spheres dealt with by the youth culture or the small group movement, although both these cultural phenomena have relevance for these oppressed groups. Their real problem is that they are shut out of history; they are victims of history, not co-creators of it. Until recently, the blacks were systematically shut out of education, politics, and economics. They were forced to be dependent upon the decisions of the white man. He was the one who shaped their historical destiny. The thrust of the black revolution has been toward the

destruction of the victim-image and the creation of a historical black man who can individually and corporately act into
history and shape his own future. This has been true in his
recent political, economic, and cultural efforts. But progress
on those fronts presupposes the change in consciousness from
a victim-image to a more positive one, and such a transformation is going on today.

The women's liberation movement as a general phenomenon bears a similar change in consciousness. Women
have always been given the run of private life and have perhaps carried the religious consciousness of the race more
adequately than men. By and large, however, they have been
barred from the public sphere. But the joys of the private
life, no matter how affluent and how "happy," cannot
assuage the basic human desire to exercise public freedom.
Not all women can want to appear in the public sphere; this
is the case with men also. But access to public action cannot
be denied a whole class of individuals. In order for access to
be gained, however, a new consciousness has had to destroy a
kind of victim-image in women that is not significantly different from that in blacks. Women have been socially conditioned to be dependent on men for the basic decisions that
control their lives. They have not been expected to use their
own freedom decisively in the public sphere—in careers,
politics, and economics. But the revolution in consciousness
will bring women into history.

We could repeat many of the same things in describing the
community organization movement. This movement, which
is basically a method for organizing and consolidating power
among the powerless, is also dependent upon a change in
consciousness. Individuals must want to determine themselves in order for the method to work. Community organizations try to call victim-oriented persons to a new stance, but
more often they are dependent on other institutions, e.g.,
churches, for the stimulation of that kind of consciousness.

The call to a new stance is not limited to cultural change among the powerless and oppressed, however. Middle class men and women also, who have not been externally oppressed, have become sensitive to the malaise of our consumer culture. The lifestyle encouraged by the mass media is one of private consumption in which the good life is seen to consist in the acquisition of more and better products. The person who adopts this lifestyle becomes another of Rieff's "psychological men," searching for pleasurable negotiations with his environment. A "floater," he does not center his life decisively in depth involvements; instead, he skims the surface of life, has a "good time," but comes down nowhere. Such a lifestyle is unsatisfying. It does not capture the greatness of each individual life, which is intimately bound up with the capacity each person has for free action in the world of history. The failure to exercise that freedom leads to despair.

The natural sciences have long used a task-oriented intentionalism in their projects, but its use in the formation and execution of policy is relatively new. Under names like "organizational development," or "process consultation," consulting groups based in academic or independent institutions are now working with church bureaucrats, corporations, faculties, boards of hospitals, etc., to help them ascertain their priorities, make the needed decisions, and execute in a systematic way the steps needed to implement their plans. These self-conscious problem-solving methods enable organizations to pull themselves out of drifting and inefficient patterns (institutions and organizations can float, too). Intentionalism as a formal methodology aids organizations in focusing themselves in order to make the greatest impact possible.

The churches participate in this cultural impulse as well as in the youth culture and the small group movement. Most of the major denominations now have a staff of experts in organizational development who use their skills to help various agencies, boards, and congregations of the churches become more intentional. These staffs apply methods that have proved successful in business to the problems of church renewal. The ambiguities of this practice are clear. Can a methodology of intentionalism operate successfully if the self-conscious decision to live intentionally on behalf of the mission of the church is absent? The methodology without the stance will lead only to peripheral improvements. Also, it is not clear that methods applicable to business will work in voluntary organizations.

Be these ambiguities as they may, the cultural movement toward intentionalism is having a significant effect on both church and society. Individuals and institutions are being called to use the freedom and greatness they possess. Such a vital new impulse can only be welcomed. It is precisely the kind of cultural movement needed for man's next step to maturity. For man can no longer allow his society to drift. He has to take charge of his own history.

Of course, the dangers of this movement are also clear. Both aspects of intentionalism, as a stance and as a methodology, are completely formal. They can be linked to any purpose, goal, or principle. Perhaps the most intentional institutions are those related to war. They do plan for the future and they successfully realize their projects. This is why a cultural phenomenon as potent as task-oriented intentionalism must be wedded to principles that press toward human fulfillment, for it can obviously be used for other purposes.

Moreover, too strong a goal-orientation sometimes makes men blind to the possibilities latent in dynamic situations. The single-mindedness of intentional persons and organizations can lead to a destructive forcing of models on a resistant or unsuitable reality. Consultants who have one main model for church renewal and who press it with great force on a congregation, may find that in their insistence on that model they have missed some of the unique gifts of the congregation. And if the congregation is resistant to their efforts, both the model and the unique gifts will be lost.

Finally, if intentionalism focuses too exclusively on the responsibility pole of lifestyle, the being pole may be neglected. Persons may be constantly summoned to pour out their being for a cause without adequate attention being given to maintenance, care, and nurture. Cups must be filled as well as poured out.

We have now finished our examination of three impulses in contemporary culture that are effecting changes in lifestyle for significant numbers of people. The youth culture, the small group movement, and task-oriented intentionalism have all been briefly described and reflected upon. The question now becomes: How do we make sense of these phenomena? Are they simply momentary flashes that will go their own separate ways and disappear? Or do they have a deeper meaning and promise? Let us now move to an interpretation, from a theological point of view, of both our present social situation, as analyzed in Chapter 1, and the three cultural emergents in relation to that situation.

The aim of the first two chapters was to communicate an awareness of what is going on in our society. First, we maintained that the economic, political, ecological, and cultural realities of contemporary American society are such that they press toward a cultural revolution for their improvement. We then discussed critically three emerging cultural impulses that are creating an undertow in American consciousness: the youth culture, with its religious-expressive dynamic; the small group movement, with its enablement of intimacy; and task-oriented intentionalism, with its stance and methodology generating historical decisiveness.

The awareness stage is not enough, however. We must press onward to an interpretation of these realities, if indeed they are realities. What do they mean from a deeper and broader perspective? If the phenomenologists are correct in arguing that man is in essence a meaning-creating agent, then it is imperative that we give a meaning to the phenomena we have described.

This critique of the awareness of certain realities is not at all foreign to the approach of theologians such as Richard and Reinhold Niebuhr, Bernard Meland, and Paul Tillich. In their reflections, the first step is to ask "What is going on?" rather than to begin with specific deductions from theological traditions or the Bible. In classical "liberal" theology, the liberal element is the approach toward belief rather than the content of belief. Experience is always the primary datum, but the awareness of experience is given a critique, an interpretation, that deepens, enriches, and amplifies the experience itself. We will use this approach in attempting to give meaning to the realities we have already described.

Naturally, one does not come empty-handed to onrushing experience. One brings to it images, concepts, thought patterns, symbols, and myths. Interpretation is the creative interplay between experience as it comes and the images, symbols, and myths that enable one to interpret it. The forms of the images, myths, and symbols are filled with content by every new experience. In this creative interaction, the symbols and myths retain and increase their meaning-giving power and the experience itself is enriched and deepened.

In this chapter we will be using the traditional symbol, "God," to enable us to give a deeper interpretation of contemporary experience. In recent centuries, the symbol has lost its evocative power because it was divorced from man's experience of the everyday world. First, during the Enlightenment, it was caught up in deistic images in which God was the great watchmaker, withdrawn and distant, who created an orderly world ruled by likewise orderly rational laws. This God was unavailable to man's experience and that particular projection of God has nearly died out.

Later, the symbol "God" was used to refer to the unexplained or uncontrollable happenings in the world. This projection, too, was divorced from the level of common experience and it is likewise in the process of dying, as has been dramatically pointed out by the Death-of-God theologians. It does not follow, however, because these particular projections of God have died, that the symbol itself is dead. On the contrary, recent theology has reshaped and reformed the symbol in order to locate its interpretive capacity much closer to the center of human experience. With these new projections, which are by no means final or eternal themselves, the traditional symbol has regained some of its old power.

Paul Tillich, among others, has asserted that the symbol is the only way man has of expressing his ultimate concern, which is the dimension of depth and breadth that we have been talking about. By outlining what Tillich sees as the function of symbols, we can perhaps better define the word "symbol" itself. First, a symbol points beyond itself to something else. It has this in common with a "sign." For instance, the American flag points beyond itself to the nation it symbolizes. Second, a true symbol, unlike a sign, participates in the reality to which it points. Again, the flag is a case in point. It participates in the power and dignity of the nation and thereby has a sanctity of its own. The deliberate destruction of a flag by demonstrators is a blasphemous deed to persons who still regard the flag as a true symbol of a great nation.

Third, a symbol opens up levels of reality in the world about us that otherwise would be closed to us. Tillich points to paintings and poems that "reveal elements of reality which cannot be approached scientifically." These artistic symbols express depth that simple description, no matter how accurate, cannot communicate. A painting such as Van Gogh's "Starry Night," with its swirling stars and twisting church spires done in deep purples and bright yellows, communicates more enchantment than a photograph can. Fourth, a symbol not only opens up dimensions and elements in the world about us but also unlocks dimensions and elements in our own soul that correspond to the dimensions and elements of the reality outside. Both the subrational and suprarational elements of our nature are tapped by powerful symbols. The painting by Van Gogh elicits the feelings of mystery, wonder, and awe in us that correspond to the startling beauty of the starry night. We cannot become aware of these elements of our soul except through symbols.

Fifth, Tillich rightly states that symbols cannot be produced intentionally. They grow out of the individual and collective unconscious and cannot function without being accepted by the unconscious dimension of our being. Symbols cannot be manufactured. Finally, symbols grow and die like living beings. They grow when the consciousness of a people is conducive to them and die when they no longer fit a new consciousness. The symbol of the "king" is a good example. It cannot possibly elicit the response it once did, the social and political role that kings play having been reduced drastically.

Myths are symbols tied together in a narration. They give an active dimension to symbols. Symbols plumb the depths and myths convey patterns of action that, although ensconced in the categories of time, actually transcend time and point to the eternal. Both symbols and myths, in their own ways, open up levels of reality that remain closed to scientific, rational description and analysis. This approach is in contrast to the popular misuse of terms like "myth" in which "myth" means a fanciful but untrue story. A myth *is* a story and though it may or may not be grounded in historical fact, it always points to a different kind of truth about the world and man than does objective, scientific language. The story of the Exodus, for example, grounded perhaps in a kernel of fact but expanded to mythic dimensions, has already been used in the introduction to this book to interpret what is happening to us as a church and as a society. In this chapter that interpretation will be amplified and elaborated.

It is extremely important for a religious community to use its symbols to interpret the signs of the times. A cogent illumination of the contemporary situation is one way that religious symbols maintain credibility and the ability to penetrate the broader society. Theologians such as Reinhold Niebuhr and Paul Tillich have preserved and extended the power of the Christian symbols by using them to criticize contemporary history and culture. Moreover, as we have already argued, theological reflection itself is done best in the midst of heightened awareness of what is going on. The religious dimension is the dimension of depth that underlines that heightened awareness. We do not exercise our religious symbols on the peripheral gaps, but right in the midst, of personal and social life.

An elemental myth in the Judeo-Christian tradition has been the exodus myth. Although the exodus from Egypt is the central shaping event of the myth, the exodus motif itself appears repeatedly in biblical literature. The calling of Abraham to a new land, the orders given to Jonah to go to a strange city, and the call of Jesus from a simple and secure life in Nazareth to a strange public ministry in Jerusalem are but a few of the examples. The myth conveys several important "moments," moments that are experienced by every individual and society in their own lives. The first moment is the *mastered world.* A mastered world is one that fits together: a man (or a society) has been able to impose an order upon his (or its) world. The divergent aspects of life have been relatively unified. It is a comfortable time, a secure time, and when it is past we remember it nostalgically. Unfortunately, such a mastered world soon becomes stagnant. The order and security soon become a kind of psychological bondage in which risk and possibility, and therefore growth, are diminished.

Individuals and societies cannot long remain within their mastered worlds. Pressures of new possibilities from within themselves, unpredictable events in the external world, claims of persons or other societies, and built-in limitations and contradictions shatter it. This shattering of our mastered worlds is accompanied both by terror and hope. When Moses led the children of Israel out of Egypt, there is little doubt that there was real trauma among the people. The event was no doubt a mixture of exhilaration and fear, and those unable to take such a shattering probably elected to remain in Egypt.

The second moment, the exodus itself, is a period of dynamic expanding movement. After the decision to leave the mastered world and to embark in freedom toward the unknown, there is great exhilaration and hope. The latent potentials kept under wraps in the mastered world are expressed. Creative chaos ensues. Certainly this was the experience of the children of Israel. Free from the bondage of Egypt, the latent religious and political impulses of an oppressed people exploded in a spontaneous way.

After the exodus, however, one must wrestle with a new situation for the self or the nation. An effort must be made to reconstitute the world, to put it back together. This is the third moment of the exodus pattern. Direction and bearings must be regained, disparate elements must be pulled together, an integrated center must be forged. All of this must be done, moreover, in the face of experiences that are not manageable. Indeed, the person or society becomes a new entity as it embraces more of life's experiences. This process, though exceedingly painful, is also the source of growth and creativity, for it is in the struggle with the shattering forces that one responds with freedom and vitality. So it was with Israel. She became a new people as she wandered in the wilderness after a shattering exodus in search of the Promised Land. The question of identity and direction became a very important one. But in embracing and living through idolatry, confusion, leadership struggle, harrassing tribes, God's never-relenting demands, etc., Israel became a new and stronger people, more fit to enter and conquer the Promised Land when it was reached. The way to renewed life is through the narrow passage of exodus, out from a mastered world. God shapes his people as a potter shapes his pot. This vivid image of Jeremiah reinforces the exodus motif, pointing as it does to the grinding and trimming of the Lord as he makes them a fit instrument of his will.

The mythic consciousness assumed that it was God behind the forces that fractured the mastered world, that called the people out. It was God who opened up the world to new possibilities. But, in contrast to a good share of present-day religious consciousness, the opening up was not a highly pleasurable, mountain-top experience. For Israel, God pressed his people through the narrow passage, the chastening fire, and that was no lark.

This powerful thrust that breaks up mastered worlds and presses toward new possibilities amid new struggles operates not only in the human, social world. It has been present in the natural world's evolution, constantly pushing toward more complexity and higher forms. The transitions from inorganic to organic, from simple one-celled to complex mutations, from fish to animal to man, are instances of mastered worlds being shattered in the great evolutionary ascent. Nikos Kazantzakis, in his *Report to Greco*, catches this dynamic in the following poetic expression.

> Blowing through heaven and earth, and in our hearts and the heart of every living thing, is a gigantic breath—a great Cry—which we call God. Plant life wished to continue its motionless sleep next to stagnant waters, but the Cry leaped up within it and violently shook its roots: 'Away, let go of the earth, walk!' Had the tree been able to think and judge, it would have cried, 'I don't want to. What are you urging me to do? You are demanding the impossible!' But the Cry, without pity, kept shaking its roots and shouting, 'Away, let go of the earth, walk!'
>
> It shouted in this way for thousands of eons; and lo! as a result of desire and struggle, life escaped the motionless tree and was liberated.
>
> Animals appeared—worms—making themselves at home in water and mud. 'We're just fine here,' they said. 'We have peace and security; we're not budging!'
>
> But the terrible Cry hammered itself pitilessly into their loins. 'Leave the mud, stand up, give birth to your betters!'
>
> 'We don't want to! We can't!'
>
> 'You can't, but I can. Stand up!'
>
> And lo! after thousands of eons, man emerged, trembling on his still unsolid legs.

The human being is a centaur; his equine hoofs are planted in the ground, but his body from breast to head is worked on and tormented by the merciless Cry. He has been fighting, again for thousands of eons, to draw himself, like a sword, out of his animalistic scabbard. He is also fighting—this is his new struggle—to draw himself out of his human scabbard. Man calls in despair, 'Where can I go? I have reached the pinnacle, beyond is the abyss.' And the Cry answers, 'I am beyond. Stand up!' All things are centaurs. If this were not the case, the world would rot into inertness and sterility.

The immense journey from the mud to the moon was pressed forward by the great Cry, as were Adam, Abraham, Moses, David, Jesus, and others throughout history. The particular point at which we stand, between the roaring sixties and the uncertain seventies is met by cries, "Allow us to rest after our world has been shattered! We can't put it back together in a new way! We can't become the new species of man we are called to be in the seventies!" But the Cry will not relent; it pressures us forward into the wilderness.

We can sketch this pressure point of God in the following diagram:

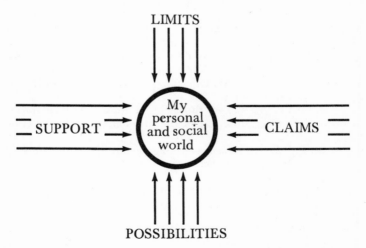

The diagram refers to the human, rather than the natural world, but it applies both to individuals and societies. The set of arrows shooting upward from below refer to the pressures of our possibilities. The desire to love, to achieve, to find truth, to play, to express oneself, to be free, to gain recognition, to forge out one's identity in relation to others, etc., are all instances of undeniable pressures that well up from within the depths of our being. Sometimes they are twisted and perverted by our own human cussedness, but nevertheless the pressures are certainly there in every person in every place. The power behind, yet in and through, these pressures is what we point to by the symbol God. The Ground of our being, God, erupts within us in our possibilities.

The second set of arrows descending toward the circle are the pressures of our limitations. Our limitations come both from within our own being and also from the external world. We have certain personality structures, shaped by heredity, environment, and our own decisions, that work against our possibilities. The desire to express oneself is met in some individuals by a personal style dominated by repression so that warmth and spontaneity cannot be expressed. The need to play is limited by work that has to be done for survival and achievement. Uncontrollable events break into personal history in ways that frustrate and limit the upward drives. Above all, the passing of time limits the upward motion of our possibilities. The past becomes the present becomes the future in a process that is not in our hands. The desire to achieve one's highest potential is limited by time's passing. One's *finis* comes before one's *telos* is reached.

The power behind those limiting, descending arrows is also God. Again, God cannot be identified in a simple-minded way with many of the limitations that meet us, but he participates as the conditioning power in all of them. We confront the limiting power of God most especially when we confront the passage of time. For at the same time that God drives us toward the eternal, he limits us in death. Every achievement is either negated or eroded by the acids of time. In fact, there is not enough time to respond adequately to all the pressures for possibility that one has within him.

When these upward and downward thrusts meet in our own being, our worlds, so carefully mastered, begin to crack. The world of childhood and adolescence is shattered by the pressure to find a serious vocation appropriate to one's gifts. The achievement of one's vocation is limited by the coming of old age. Our lives are a series of putting worlds together, having them shattered by possibilities and limitations, and struggling to put them together in new ways, embracing more of the pain and joy of life in those struggles. The power behind these pressures is the great Cry, merciless and relentless.

The arrows coming from the right hand side of the diagram designate the claims and resistance that others put upon us. (The horizontal arrows apply to the interpersonal world.) The children that demand attention and love, the spouse who insists upon treatment as an independent being, the friend who needs help, the person with whom one just can not get along, etc., all represent claims and resistance upon us. They come to us in our lives and demand response. That also cracks our orderly worlds. Persons who show up in our lives lure or sometimes force us out of one situation in life into another. Marriage and the coming of children are examples. And the power behind these claims is God. For what are these claims from others except the pressures of their own possibilities being aimed in our direction? The demand of children for attention and love is simply the other side of their drive toward significance and love. When we meet the claims and resistance of others, we are put on God's pressure point. Again, these claims cannot be identified in any simple way with God's intentions because many times they are perverted and twisted by the person through whom they are coming. But, nevertheless, the spoiled child's overweening demands are at root empowered by a good impulse toward love and significance. That impulse is motivated by God.

Finally, the arrows from the left side of the diagram refer to the support one receives from others. For others buoy one up in life, filling one's cup so that one can survive and achieve. Without them one would have no real identity, no real "place" in life. But they also enable one to take part in life and therefore they do put one on the pressure point. Again, the power behind these forces is God. He is holding one up through the love and concern that erupts in and through other persons.

All of these taken together constitute the web of life— complex, confusing, terrifying, wonderful, latent with possibility and death. Fortunately, they seem to connive to turn the screws sharply only at certain times. Much of life takes place in a mastered world. But we are pressured out of it, broken open to new challenges, problems, struggles. God will not let us go.

As Bultmann has it:

> It is God who makes man finite, and who makes a comedy of man's care, who allows his longing to miscarry, who casts him into solitude, who sets a terminus to his knowing and doing, who calls him to duty, and who gives the guilty over to torment. And yet at the same time it is God who forces man into life and drives him into care; who puts longing and the desire to love in his heart; who gives him thoughts and strength for his work, and who places him in the eternal struggle between self-assertion and duty. God is the enigmatic power beyond time, yet master of the temporal, beyond being, yet working in it.

When the pressure point diagram is applied to a whole society, the arrows then stand for huge social movements and historical events that are obviously corporate in nature. The temporal sequence in movement from a mastered to a shattered world is marked in decades or generations—sometimes even centuries.

We have already indicated our conviction that the decade of the fifties was an instance of a mastered world in American history. Our world then seemed to fit together. It was calm and orderly, perhaps even placid. The Korean War was ended and Eisenhower, a fatherly non-political figure, presided over a country that sought surcease from conflict and war. After Joe McCarthy, Congress settled down to an unspectacular period. College campuses experienced nothing more disruptive than panty raids, which had very little political content. The racial problem had not yet surfaced with power although it was foreshadowed when troops were sent to Little Rock. The youth, while critical to some extent, did not act out their feelings in an organized way. Popular music was dominated by the sentimental love ballad. The Cold War was always on but it did not seem to disturb society unduly. Sputnik went up in 1957, but it was several years before a renewed American emphasis on the natural sciences was felt. All in all, it was a good time, a comfortable time. Those who grew up then, adults in their thirties now, did not experience the ruptures of culture and society that the current young have. Most accepted the American Dream and its more tarnished reality, and the minority who criticized both remained within the liberal, reformist tradition. Utopianism was definitely not in vogue and revolutionary consciousness was something that happened in Europe. This mastered world, with its tendencies toward secure bondage, is nowadays the object of waves of nostalgia.

God would not allow such a pause to continue. The smoldering fires that were kept under wraps burst out, and the flames came as both possibility and limitation. The upward shooting arrows of our diagram were numerous. The desire of blacks for dignity and equal treatment, certainly a product of God's upward pressing power, gained momentum. The civil rights and then the Black Power movements were and remain eruptions of God's good power. (This is not to say that some of the good impulses were not distorted. As is always the case, human sin twists even the best efforts of men. But the distortions produced by the underdog are always more understandable and justifiable than those of the favored.) The pressure of these upward surges broke open our society to great new possibilities that have been shared by black, white, red, and brown alike.

The surge of black people for their rightful place in society has been experienced not only as possibility, but also as limitation—the descending arrows in our diagram. That is, the power of God operating through the black revolution has come as judgment upon white people and their institutions. Blacks have told us in a thousand different ways what kind of a society we have and what kind of a people we have been. Such hard truth has a shattering effect on a mastered world. Judgment and possibility are inextricably bound together as God generates a movement toward freedom within the depths of an oppressed people. The ambiguity of this process is only increased by the recalcitrance and insensitivity of whites and the abuse of the movement by some blacks. (The black movement has occasionally been used for illegitimate private gain, sometimes merely the psychological gain that accompanies the wholesale denunciation of whites and sometimes an economic gain when blackness is used as a lever for near extortion.)

White society has by now been broken open to new and increased entrance for blacks, but the battle is certainly not over. There is still a huge pool of black people who are disabled and/or shut out, and they will continue to smolder even if the fireworks of the sixties are not repeated in the seventies. Certainly the black revolution, coming as both judgment and possibility, has participated in God's pressure point. It has shattered our mastered world and forced us to repent, to define ourselves and respond in new ways. We are not yet exactly sure what the proper definition and response is—and that is part of our wilderness experience. All we can say is that it will never be the same. The great Cry presses onward.

We could elaborate in much the same way the efforts of the New Left, women's liberation, consumer protection agencies, ecological organizations, Indian and Chicano groups, and community organizations. All would have similar profiles. They have come as both judgment and possibility, and all have a para-political style.

Certain other pressures operating in contemporary life need to be pointed out separately, however, for they have cracked open wide fissures in our world.

The technological revolution, perhaps the single most important source of social change today, is continually expanding the possibilities of life in the 20th century. We need think only of the revolutions in medical care, transportation, communication, production, farming, building, etc., to see how much potential there is for a better life for all. But the dark side of the technological revolution is exercising its own kind of judgment upon our society. Unplanned technological expansion has altered our environment drastically. Great populations have been forced off the land into already overcrowded urban areas. Given our technological ability to create ever bigger machines and vehicles, it is clear that when mistakes are made or break-downs occur the consequences are ponderous. (Witness here the cracking up of giant oil tankers and the resultant prodigious spillage.)

Technology has enabled us to raise three-fifths of our population to relative affluence, but it has also depressed one-fifth of our population by destroying low-skilled jobs in precisely those areas where there are a lot of poor. Technological development has also widened the gap between the rich and the poor nations—the rich get richer and the poor get poorer. Again, the use of a potent technology has caught our society in a squeeze. The God-driven desire in man's soul to understand and control has led to technological revolution, and God's pressures, working through human agency, have again put us on the pressure point, and have shattered our orderly world.

The developing Third World's striving for nationhood and for an adequate standard of living hits us right in the face. Besides the claims made upon us for aid and support (the horizontal arrows from the right), the Third World is declaring for economic and political self-determination. For us, that means not simply staying out of a country with our money and influence; it also means stepping out in greater or lesser degrees, or at least allowing local control over our enterprises there. Whether we can withdraw our economic and political tentacles gracefully is a serious question. Our tragic and painful involvement in Vietnam should have taught us that efforts toward national liberation, whether strictly nationalist, communist, or a mixture, have a certain irresistible force. America, a land with a revolutionary tradition, now finds itself lined up against revolutions. What a shattering blow—not only in terms of our own national morale, but also in terms of lost lives, lost unity, lost money, and lost hopes. As many ambiguities as there are in the history of the Vietnam War, we still cannot doubt that underneath it all is the struggle of a people to be free. And the power behind that struggle for freedom is the power of the Lord. Once again, he has put us on the pressure point, and as this war winds down, the question for this decade becomes: What will be the stance of the United States when the dozens of inevitable revolutions break out?

Perhaps the most shattering of God's arrow is neither of the above. Perhaps that is simply our mortality, by virtue of which the finite amount of energy and resolve granted us is slowly drained away. America has lived through a time of accelerating change such as has never been seen before. She has carried millions of European peasants in the womb of her great cities and reared them right into the suburbs. The cities, their schools, their organizations, their transportation, their buildings, are tired. Within the space of two short centuries, America has lived the lifetime of several nations. And now, in a moment of tiredness, she finds herself hit by a black revolution, a women's revolution, and near ecological disaster. Can she respond? Or has the Lord of history ground her down as he has done to so many nations and empires?

The cultural impetus for those two centuries has been the bourgeois lifestyle. Without playing down in a nonsensical way the strong points of such a lifestyle, its discipline, energy, and rationality, we can say that its central thread, its privatistic and individualistic acquisitiveness, will not carry our society into a better future. Indeed, as Ferkiss has argued, having bourgeois man at the helm of the technological society invites disaster. Not only is that lifestyle inappropriate to the great responsibility that lies ahead, it also does not adequately meet the basic needs of people. The needs of communal intimacy (depth), religious expression (mystery), and a significant use of one's freedom (greatness) are not met by such a lifestyle. It may have been appropriate to one kind of world and indeed may have felt at home as it mastered it. But that world has been shattered by the Lord of history himself, and the exhausted lifestyle that attended that world will have to go too. God has once again pushed us out of our secure bondage into an exodus that so far has led us only into a wilderness, and once again we must decide who we really are.

It seems apparent that the years from 1965-70 have been particularly a period of increased pressure on our society and on the individuals within it. The shattering process focused on that stretch of time. In addition to the structural alignments that militate for a moderate, if not conservative course (the majority of Americans are, after all, middle class and relatively comfortable), there has also been an attitudinal shift toward the political center. The pressure exerted upon individuals by the breaking-open process has already been enough for them to want the putting-together process to begin. Many on the left who flirted with radicalism have either dropped out (the cynical response) or become more realistic about the pace of political change and about the effectiveness of revolutionary rhetoric and organizations. The working class, which has at times been attracted to George Wallace, has moved more toward its traditional stance since the economic slow-down. By and large, the political vectors indicate that a decade of moderate politics lies ahead. With the political and economic world dampened, the coming years will be a crucial period in which to build the new cultural consciousness that will eventually unfold into economic and political activity.

Let us conclude this chapter by raising this question: What in fact have we gained by interpreting the present social crisis through the traditional Christian symbol, God? If it is true that a religious community must make sense of its world in terms of its symbols, what credible insights have emerged in the foregoing interpretation?

First, let us take one of the main functions of a religious symbol: it opens up dimensions in the world that are otherwise hidden. Under this rubric we would propose three important insights.

1. There is a profound meaning in the challenges and struggles we are confronting. Even though our secure world has been shattered and our future is uncertain, we are not caught in an inevitable ebb and flow of senseless organic cycles, to which the natural response would be a stoical resignation. The shoving out of a mastered world into an exodus is part of the Great Ascent. Kazantzakis's worm pleaded, "We're just fine here in the mud; we have peace and security; we're not budging." But the terrible Cry shattered their comfortable world of mud and water. So it is with us at this time. The

great furnace of endless energy is pressing forward in the upward-sweeping process of personalization. The power is pushing toward the fulfillment of human community that can only come through the narrow passage of struggle. Our significant gift and terrible burden is that we are living in a time in which the dynamics of the Lord seem to be accelerating. The dialectic is increasing in intensity. Either something wonderfully attractive or awe-fully frightening lies at the threshold of the future. Reality cannot bear much more muddling through.

2. The emergents we have pointed to by using arrows standing for possibility, limitation, support, and claims, are the agents through which God exercises his power. The small group movement, the youth culture, intentionalism, the Vietnam War, the black revolution, etc., all participate in God's pressure point. When we meet them we not only respond to particular human agents, we also respond to the pressures of God. They are part of the Cry. *But none of them can be identified completely or simply with God's will.* None of them is God's new messiah. In secular language, none of them is *the* answer to the whole struggle. Each, after all, is finite. They live and die; they flourish for a time and then are passed by. Only the Lord is constant in intent and power. Moreover, each of these agents is also tainted by the distortions and perversions of man's own tendency to make himself the center of meaning and power.

The proletariat, the black revolution, the peace movement, the youth culture—none of these are sinless, none can be expected to save us. If any of them ever garnered enough power to try to do so, it would be prone to the same corruptions as that of the "establishment." In fact, its leaders would perhaps be more dangerous than the cynical establishment precisely because they are likely to be more self-righteous.

3. The power behind the pressure point we experience comes to us first as the *enemy*. The Lord of History is the

destroyer of men and their comfortable worlds. He is particularly active in the midst of the struggle between the old and the new. For it is he who turns the screws on us. This insight is very hard for many American church people to accept because they have been reared with the near heretical notion that God is only associated with "good" experiences. But our fathers in the faith knew differently. Israel saw the hand of God in the conflict of nations and in her own fall, both of them replete with plenty of human suffering. Jesus saw God's pressure point for him clearly in Gethsemane. Luther argued that God comes to us first as Law, not as Gospel. And the Law is more than simply a painful conscience; it is the pressure point of God. It is made up of all those pressures that impinge upon us—limitations, possibilities, support, and claims. Sometimes it is open possibility, and sometimes sheer hell. Interestingly, it comes most powerfully to us when we are under the greatest pressure. Then we are tempted, as Luther, to curse God who will not let us go, and who shapes us on his potter's wheel. When we experience God in this way, his power is evident, but his goodness is not. We experience the dark side of God mixed maddeningly with his providence.

Each of these insights into the nature of the world elicits a corresponding insight into our own souls. Symbols lift up realities within our own persons that are not evident otherwise. Such insights include the following:

1. If it is true that the world of struggle outside is a meaningful one, it is also true that humans are enabled to participate in those struggles with more vitality if they are convinced that their efforts are consonant with the movement of reality itself. As one man put it after describing the nature of his own pressure point, "If I can really believe that it is God that I am wrestling with, then my struggles are bearable and meaningful." Human strivings can be borne if they are anchored in a meaningful story.

2. The tendency in the world for new movements to invest themselves with undue significance is matched in the human soul with a tendency to reach for false security. Before the pressure point, a likely response is to fasten oneself to the latest thing that shows promise. So we have the true believers in the black revolution who see it as *the* saving instrument of God. Charles Reich sees Consciousness III, that of the youth culture, as the only redemptive agent of a dying society. But we must beware of this tendency in our souls and stand illusionless before the flaming inferno that destroys all idols in its burning ascent.

3. As we meet God as enemy in the world about us, the response in our inner beings is to escape. We can try to escape the pressure point by geographical means—leave the city, get out of the hot kitchen. Or we can try psychological escapes. One of these is to insist that things are really not so different now than they were, and that our old approaches will still work. Another is to blame others or institutions for our plight. Scape-goating is a favorite game among persons confronted by the pressure point. At any rate, when the screws are turned and the power behind life seems to make conditions intolerable, we do anything to lessen the pressure.

But the pressure will not go away. For the Lord is in our loins. He is in the world about us. He will not let go of us. We may yell and scream, but the God of the law is always there, pressing us with that from which we run frantically—our own mystery, depth, and greatness. He presses us to decide. Shall I live or die? If one decides to die, not physically but figuratively, he hounds him with a despair that can come only to creatures who at root really are great. If one tries to live according to his possibility as a mysterious, deep, and great creature, he finds himself alienated from the very strengths of his being. One cannot liberate himself. God the law only teaches us our alienated state. He does not solve our problems for us.

FOUR

The present decade confronts us with this question: Can the church find an appropriate and authentic role for itself in such a period of uncertainty? Can it renew itself and its mission in the midst of an atmosphere of demoralization and retrenchment? The same challenge that confronts society confronts the church also. Can it live on the pressure point of the Lord? Can it be a creative part of a cultural revolution?

As we attempt this renewal of life and mission, we find that the chastening fire of the Lord has already separated us from some of our fond perversions. The social-ethical perversion, which mistakenly identified social action as the central mission of the church, is only now dying a painful death. Adherents of this point of view are already leaving the church for agencies and organizations more clearly defined for social action. The psychological perversion, which saw the church as an oasis for small group work and where each person was justified by his brother's strokes, is clearly not going to win the day either. As for the intellectualistic perversion, which sees the church as an ideological community defending written propositions, it is dying the death of progressive fragmentation.

So, what is the church's mission? What is our unique role in this new situation? It is the same as it always has been—the proclamation of the word of God. This function has been displaced, shunted aside, perverted, and overlooked, but never quite lost. To say that it is the same as always is deceptive, however, because the word always has to be appropriated and proclaimed in new forms that will penetrate modern consciousness. The word is always addressed to the inner man—and such address is a fiendishly difficult task. It is easier to lapse into defining the mission of the church in ways that are more visible and amenable to manipulation. These easier ways are always built on the false assumption that man's basic problem lies outside himself, in his situation. The central problem facing man, however, is his relation to the situation. The pressure point of the Lord is God the law demanding that man decide who he is and what relation he is going to take before life as it comes to him. God the law is hard. He drives men and nations to the edge. He breaks them open, forcing the question of life or death.

The good word that the church bears, and this defines its central mission, is that the grace of God can and does erupt in the midst of the pressure point experience. Our fathers in the faith asserted this miracle of life by announcing the good news that God's mercy trancends his judgment, and that his grace overflows his law.

In order to point to and illuminate this eruption of grace in life we must resort again to symbol. Here the second great symbol of the Christian faith comes into play, the symbol of Jesus Christ. This symbol is anchored in history by the life, death, and resurrection of Jesus of Nazareth, but as a symbol it points beyond itself to something that transcends the particular history in which it appeared. Jesus Christ points to God's liberating grace that erupts in life according to God's will. The Christ-Word (the symbol) points to, participates in, and illuminates the Christ-Event (the experience). The word of God, given to us historically in the story of Jesus Christ, is the fullest manifestation of the experience and the further communication of liberating grace. Because we are the witnesses to that fullest manifestation in a configuration of historical events—Jesus' life, death, and resurrection—the church has been given the interpretative symbol that gives meaning and depth to the experience of liberating grace wherever and whenever it occurs.

Most persons experience the stroke of liberating grace in less than dramatic ways. Sometimes the significance of the event is not even grasped at the moment; only later on, in reflection and re-living, is the effect of the event finally realized. For many persons, liberation comes in series of smaller events, not in once and for all pivotal changes. But the experience of liberating grace is a definite and describable human experience. When it comes, whether great or small, it comes in four aspects that take on the shape of the Christ-Word. For the Christ-Event (the experience) has a shape or logos that we have called the Christ-Word (the symbol). Let us put this into a diagram.

All is
Good

The past
is approved

The future
is open

You are
accepted

First, in explicating our diagram, we want to re-emphasize that the stroke of liberating grace takes place in the midst of life. This St. Andrew's cross is superimposed upon the pressure point of God. Liberation comes in the midst of life, not on its periphery.

The top section—All is Good—is easier to express in song or poetry. It is the simple religious experience that affirms that, in spite of all, life is good. "I will take the whole loaf of life as it comes, hulls and pits as well as the nutritious parts, and bite into it with all my being." It is the affirmation that the heart of reality is basically for us and not against us. Life can be responded to with trust. This is not sentimentalism: it fully and without illusion recognizes the tragedy and pain that is a part of the loaf of life. But it gathers up the negative into a basically positive response to a basically positive reality. My situation as it comes to me can be affirmed because it is in the hand of God. I accept the given of my life and all life with trust.

This first aspect has a universal dimension to it. It embraces the world. The second aspect, however, is aimed directly at the person in all his particularity. It proclaims: "You are fundamentally OK." Not you are OK *if* you do this or that. Rather, you are fundamentally OK just as you are. You are suitable to live in your situation. With all your limits and possibilities you are just the one for it. Accept yourself as a worthwhile person with your own unique mystery, depth, and greatness. Thus, the stroke of liberating grace enables one to appropriate the adequacy of one's own being in the context of an accepting ground of all being.

The third and fourth aspects have a temporal dimension to them. The left-hand quadrant refers to the past, its real or imagined chains. For most persons, the past includes not only events and persons who injured or hindered them, but also things that *they* did and feel guilty about. In both cases, the past strangles the capacity for people to live their lives with decisiveness.

The stroke of liberating grace frees one from the weight of the past. Our fathers in the faith called this "the forgiveness of sins" and they understood the potency of freedom from the chains of the past. The weight of the past is not only taken off in the experience of grace, but the past can be accepted. One no longer has to shove it into dark places in the mind and heart where it can control life by unconscious tugs. After all, that particular, concrete past has brought us to the present moment where grace is real. No other past has done it, only this one.

The fourth aspect of the logos or structure of the Christ-Event refers to the future. In the moment of grace, the future is open. Whereas a moment before the pressures of life seemed to create an inpenetrable wall, the stroke of grace makes clear that the future is not determined. It is open, amenable to the decisions that one can make right now. It can be shaped. In short, one is not a victim of a grinding inevitability.

Several things need to be reiterated in regard to this stroke of liberating grace, this Christ-Event.

First, it does not change the external situation. It transforms the inner man, and the stance he takes before the situation. In one sense, nothing is changed but in another, everything is. By virtue of this new stance, one has the resources to begin to shape the external situation. He can use his life decisively because he is in touch with its power.

Second, the event of grace may come without any religious tag on it. It may happen without reflective awareness and it may be mediated by all sorts of agents. It may come through a shattering event, a casual word from a friend, a proclaimed word from a pulpit, or a "cup of cold water" from an unexpected source. But though the liberating grace comes *through* these agents, it is always something more than them. God uses them as vehicles for his powerful thrust into the center of human will and personality, and because they are only vehicles, they cannot control the stroke of grace. God alone is the controller of his liberating gifts. None of us can guarantee liberation. We can only try to become vehicles of it.

A question that is raised by the last point presents itself. If the stroke of grace can occur without any explicit religious awareness, what indeed is the role of the church? Even prior to that, what is the role of Jesus Christ? In order to explain, we must use a biblical story.

> Then he made the disciples get into the boat and go before him to the other side, while he dismissed the crowds. And after he had dismissed the crowds, he went up into the hills by himself to pray. When evening came, he was there alone, but the boat by this time was many furlongs distant from the land, beaten by the waves; for the wind was against them. And in the fourth watch of the night he came to them, walking on the sea. But when the disciples saw him walking on the sea, they were terrified, saying, "It is a ghost!" And they cried out for fear. But immediately he spoke to them, saying, "Take heart, it is I; have no fear."
>
> And Peter answered him, "Lord, if it is you, bid me come to you on the water." He said, "Come." So Peter got out of the boat and walked on the water and came to Jesus; but when he saw the wind, he was afraid, and beginning to sink he cried out, "Lord, save me." Jesus immediately reached out his hand and caught him, saying to him, "O man of little faith, why did you doubt?" And when they got into the boat, the wind ceased. And those in the boat worshiped him, saying, "Truly you are the Son of God."   Matthew 14:28-33

On the surface, this story seems to be incapable of shedding any useful light on the meaning of grace and the church's relation to the mediation of grace. But with an accurate understanding of symbol and myth, the story takes on significant meaning for us as contemporary human beings. First, we must understand the meaning of the symbol, water, to ancient people. Water was on the one hand a primary symbol of life. Ancient peoples were very dependent upon water for the necessary sustenance of life. Its presence meant the possibility of green things, of human and animal life. Its coolness contrasted with the dry parched land so common in the Middle East. Water as a symbol thus pointed to the mysterious life-giving powers and forces in life. It pointed to vitalities in the world that were *for* man, giving him the possibility of life and happiness. The rite of baptism itself is bound up with this life-giving meaning of water.

On the other hand, water was also the symbol of death and of chaos. Although the surface of the water symbolized life, the deeps symbolized death. It was in the dark deeps that forces of evil and chaos lurked. To fall into the deeps meant to go to a horrible death. Deep water represented the dark, mysterious powers in reality that were death-dealing. In storms the death-dealing powers erupted on the surface and overcame the life-giving forces. That which was life-giving became death-dealing. The sacrament of baptism has a relation to this darker side of water symbolism, too. To be immersed in water meant to go to one's death, at least the death of one's former, unredeemed self.

When Jesus walks on the water in the story, we are being told that he could walk on life. He had so much trust in the sustaining powers of life that he could negotiate his way across the surface with confidence and decisiveness. Moreover, in the story there is a storm. Life, like a lake in a storm, is rough. The wind and the waves upset one's equilibrium. The powers of death erupt from the deeps and buffet people about. Life is not a smooth surface but sometimes turns into a rough sea that shatters one's security. Nevertheless, despite the storm with its wind and waves, Jesus maintained his confidence in the power of God that stood behind both life and death.

The final reality is trustworthy and one can walk on life with trust in and loyalty to that final reality. The references in Jesus' stories to "the lilies of the field" and "each hair of your head is numbered" all communicate this basic trust in God, the ground of all being. Because Jesus was able to live out of the faith that, indeed, all that is is good, his cup was full. He could therefore pour out his cup with decisiveness. He could *decide* where to die his death. He told Pilate in effect, "you can't take my life from me because I have already decided to give it up." Jesus was a free man, full of trust and decisive loyalty to the One, God the Father. And that is what the story of Jesus walking on the water means.

The company of Jesus was the witness to a man who lived in utter faith and loyalty. They communicated that witness through a story replete with symbols and myths.

But the end of the story of Jesus and Peter is something different. When Peter saw Jesus walking on the stormy sea of life, he said to himself, "How I would like to live my life and die my death like that! I would give anything for a life of such confidence and a death of such decisiveness!" So Peter asked Jesus for the word. And it was given: "Come on, Peter. Come into life. You can live your life and die your death in faith." And for a moment at least, Peter had faith. The stormy water of life sustained him. His faith, however, was short-lived. (Note that Jesus says to Peter after his failure, "O man of *little faith*, why did you doubt?") That which was sustaining him — water, life in the storm — became his death — water, the dark mystery of the abyss. Nevertheless, Jesus rescued him from death, reproaching him for his lack of faith. Peter had many such ups and downs, but finally it seems that his faith was strong enough so that he could die for the cause of the Lord, and that cause was the proclamation of the word about God through the church.

This story about Jesus is pregnant with meaning and significance. First of all, it tells us what the early followers of Jesus believed about him. He was a liberated zone, so to say. He walked on life and died his death. All the intentions of God for mankind were manifested in him. He is the sacrament of God, transparent to all the intentions of the Lord. He incarnated the underlying structure of reality, the logos. In the midst of the storms of alienation Jesus showed forth in flesh and blood all that God wished for the fulfillment of man. Thus, he is God's word. As *the* word, he lived out of the four aspects of grace. He was God's grace-word. He lived out of complete trust that all is good, that he was acceptable and suitable to the task that came to him in life, that his past was approved and that the future was open. For three days, from

Good Friday to Easter Sunday, the future was in doubt. But the word could not be stopped by death or the passing of time. It came alive again. Jesus the grace-word lived again. The future was indeed open for the word and for the church that followed from the word. Thus, Jesus was the Second Adam, the fulfillment of all that was a potential for the first Adam but was lost. As the disciples confessed at the end of our story, "Truly you are the Son of God."

To be sure, Jesus not only was and is the word of God for men, he also communicated it to others. He not only was a liberated zone, but he spoke the word of liberating grace for others. Peter was charged with a stupendous task for life — to be a fisher of men and a founder of the church; and in spite of Peter's spotty past, his betrayal and doubt, he was fully adequate to the task because of the liberation of Jesus' word of grace. Thus, through all the ages Jesus as the powerful word has been like a gigantic gong struck in a quiet hall. The reverberations have spread throughout history, catching people up into its shapes and contours, molding them in the shape of the word. The sound of the Christ-Word was not what a lot of persons expected or wished for. The ragged itinerant preacher who claimed to be God's word and who claimed to speak it to others, especially the poor, did not go over too well with the Zealots, who wanted a political messiah, or with the priests, who wanted a new temple-builder, or with the Pharisees and Nazarenes, who wanted a law-abiding, ascetic type. The word was an offense. It proclaimed that life came through the narrow passage. Finally, it could not be tolerated. Jesus the word was crucified as a criminal. But the word could not be killed. It came alive again. Standing this far from the event, it is hard for us to say exactly what happened. All we know is that a vivifying experience of the first order occurred. The depression and death of Good Friday became the decisiveness and vitality of Easter. The word, expressed through the lives of that small tattered band, sprang forth into all the reaches of the earth with contagious energy. Something so extraordinary happened that the early Christian community had to express it in the mythological language of resurrection and ascension.

Like many other biblical stories, the story of Jesus on the water gives us a clue to the mission of the church. The unique and essential mission of the church is the proclamation of the word that it has been given in Jesus Christ. For it is the liberating grace that the word communicates or points to that deals with *the* central problem of human life. It deals with the basic relation one has with the very ground of one's being, God himself. The real liberation, to be one's authentic self, to be reunited with the origin and aim of our lives, is the goal of the word. This task is prior in significance to all others before the church. But, as so often is the case, if the church seeks first the Kingdom of God's word, other things will be added to it. If the church can regain a sharpness in proclaiming the word of life, it can become a major shaper of the cultural revolution of the future. The stroke of liberating grace, therefore, is bound together with a conscious communication of the Christ-Word. The Christ-Word and the Christ-Event occur together. This is a self-conscious religious moment. Salvation, redemption, and liberation are words used to point to that moment and they carry with them a self-conscious relation to Jesus Christ. In many cases, however, the Christ-Event and the Christ-Word do not come together chronologically. The appropriation of the moment of liberation in retrospect is nothing new. It was only long after the exodus, for instance, that Israel gave that event the status of the liberation of God. So it may be with us. In moving through the narrow passage of death into life by the enablement of some inexplicable moment of grace, we many times experience the liberation of God without bringing that moment to conscious awareness. Many persons can point to turning-points in their lives that have the shape of the

Christ-Event, but they need the Christ-Word to give them depth and meaning and long-lasting significance. With such a convincing means of interpreting the most eventful moments of their lives, persons once more can come into contact with the power of the Christian symbols for their everyday lives.

Liberating grace, either in direct conscious connection with the Christ-Word or in interpretation in retrospect, has important effects then on one's on-going life. In the moment of grace nothing external is changed, but the stance to life is changed. God the enemy becomes God the friend. The pressure point is seen as the necessary bath of fire for new life. The uniqueness of each new moment is more sensitively apprehended. In short, one is brought into touch with the mystery of one's existence, the shrouded secrets of sin and grace. Worship becomes a real possibility.

One's relation with others is deepened. One's struggle with the Lord of life becomes everyman's struggle. Each person's infinite possibilities and complex nature are recognized and related to. The quality of interpersonal life is enhanced. One finds the resources to break through the layers of alienation that corrode human relations. Following the moment of grace, the authentic depth of human life can be appropriated.

Finally, the decisiveness of the free life becomes a possibility. The future is open and I can freely decide to thrust my life significantly into history. It may not be earth-shaking, but each life can make a difference in the stream of history. Events can be shaped. By being intentional and using my gifts and freedom decisively, I can break from the floating life and make my life count. The greatness of life is related to intentionality, the freedom to channel one's life into decisive action.

Our essential mission as the church is to finish the work of our fathers, the work established by God through Jesus Christ. This involves the care and communication of these powerful keys to the meaning of life with its pressure point and its grace and its possibilities for mystery, depth, and greatness. These symbols constitute the true word about life.

As the present body of Christ on earth, the church is called to respond to drowning people. Persons whose lives are becoming deaths, who are falling into the deeps, call out for help. The church must respond with supportive action, buoying up persons with no questions asked. This is the task of supportive grace that the human community as individuals and institutions can perform. We cannot control the operation of liberating grace, but we can intentionally communicate supportive grace. We can increase the arrows coming from the left on our pressure point diagram. That is within our ability. Involvement in the struggle for human welfare and rights is our calling as the church of Jesus Christ. The significance of such action should not be played down, for the "cup of cold water" given out of human compassion can become the occasion for the stroke of liberating grace. The Christ-Word can be acted out in deeds of justice that can elicit the Christ-Event in the lives of individuals. We cannot guarantee that, but it is a possibility that is always present. When it does happen we can only rejoice and help persons further to a conscious awareness of God's liberating grace in their lives.

In conclusion, we can hold up some of the individual and social implications of this clarity on the mission of the church. If the essential role of the church as the body of Christ relates to the interpretation and communication of the word of liberating grace, there are important consequences.

First, there are consequences for the individual. It is clear that this definition of the church's mission addresses the problem of human life where it really is: deep within the human will. There is a recurring tendency in Western culture to locate the crux of our problems in something external to man. Man himself (or at least segments of mankind) is then seen as basically innocent and sinless. If we could only get rid of private property, big business, sexual repression, white people, black people, Jews, the church, the older generation, the establishment, socialism, communism, ignorance, etc., man would be free at last. Then the sinless proletariat, communist party, sexual hedonists, black people, white people, Aryans, atheists, young people, powerless, capitalists, educators, etc., would lead us to paradise.

This list of all our demons and saviors sounds ridiculous, but it has a serious point. Man always wants to lay the blame on something or someone outside himself. Man loves to escape having to face his own alienation by scape-goating. Inner poverty of spirit is projected upon outside demons. One can live as a cripple with a grand excuse and with glorious self-righteousness. This is not to say that there is no external oppression. Of course there is, and it must be attacked and erased. But liberation always starts with a revolution in inner consciousness. The alienation of man from himself and, in Christian terms, from the ground of his being, is the crux of the problem. And Christianity, with its realism about the omnipresence of sin in *all* individuals, is the interpretation of human life most likely to address that problem without manufacturing external demons that immediately misplace the struggle. The Christian symbols, with their deep understanding of sin and grace, of life itself, address the individual where he calls out for a true word.

In addition to its implications for individuals, this understanding of the role of the church and its Christ-Word has implications of a social nature as well. No society can experience what we have called a Christ-Event. Unlike individuals, groups cannot repent and be liberated from their alienation. Claims that this has happened usually mean that the group is more alienated, in the sense that it has made itself into an idol. There is, however, in the life of a group or nation, something analogous to the Christ-Event. Though we would not go so far as to call it a stroke of liberating grace, there can be a significant change in corporate consciousness. For instance, the beginning of the end of the Depression came with the proclamation that "we have nothing to fear but fear itself." The crucial problem facing the American people at that time was rightly apprehended. It was a problem of the inner spirit, of our culture, not of a lack of external resources or ability. The President pronounced to the people the word of suitability, of affirmation.

Perhaps it is important at this time for the church to reassess its word to the larger society. In the decade of the sixties, the church found itself subjected to a sharp critique. Then the church set itself over against society. It denounced society in its handling of the racial problem, the war, the environment, and the deterioration of the cities. It participated vigorously in protest movements. None of these problems has gone away and all yet need incisive criticism. Guilty parties need to be exposed to public protest and agitation. Most of all, responsible agitation needs to be bolstered. But the consciousness of the society as a whole is more depressed than haughty or arrogant. Withering streams of denunciation and protest seem cheap and easy. Perhaps the church's new stance must be the illusionless proclamation of the word of affirmation, of suitability, to the American people. This proclamation must be illusionless, for it must not gloss over our problems nor absolve individuals of their responsibility. But it must address itself to the tendency persons have to see themselves as helpless victims who can only resign themselves to powerful demonic forces. The national pressure point, upon which God has put us, can be responded to with the death wish as well as haughty defiance. We are closer as a nation to the former than to the latter. We need the church's word of suitability in the midst of this wilderness experience.

Finally, the foregoing understanding of the nature of the church and its unique mission has implications for the social use of the new cultural impulses that are emerging in

American society. The cultural impulses that we described earlier—the youth culture, the small group movement, and intentionalism—have a tendency to claim too much for themselves. The Christian faith, however, with a more profound understanding of liberation, can enable our culture to use these cultural gifts in a more centered way. For when they are not made to carry more weight than they are able, these impulses can become great instruments in the humanization of American society. Here the church as a cultural institution *par excellence* finds a key role to play. As an institution that deals intentionally with inner consciousness, with the cultural level of life, it can become a demonstration project for the rest of society.

FIVE   TOWARD A RENEWED

LIFESTYLE

> We are faced with a spiritual conflict of the most acute kind, a sort
> of social schizophrenia which divides the soul of society between a
> non-moral will to power served by inhuman techniques and a reli-
> gious faith and a moral idealism which have no power to influence
> human life. There must be a return to unity—a spiritual integration
> of culture—if mankind is to survive.
>
> Christopher Dawson
> *Religion and Culture*, p. 217

We have now examined social dysfunctions on the one
hand, and a theological interpretation and perspective on the
other. Economic, political, ecological, and cultural problems,
many of them spin-offs of a galloping technology, represent
one-half of the social schizophrenia that Dawson refers to
above. The other half consists of some fragmentary impulses
toward renewal and the potent symbols of Christian Faith.

How do we transcend this schizophrenia? How do the fragmentary impulses find an integrating center so that they can
be coordinated for maximum impact? How can the Christian
symbols, with their meaning-giving potency, make use of
these new cultural impulses and gather the power to influence our technological society?

The key to overcoming this schizophrenia is the forging of
a new, concrete lifestyle. A strong new corporate lifestyle can
bridge the gap between a soulless technological society and a
renewed internal consciousness. Such a new lifestyle must

gather up the loose strands of the impulses toward cultural renewal we have already talked about. It must integrate them into a potent, broader vision and discipline them into a focused effort. In short, it must express the new elements of consciousness through an effective social vehicle. The church's role as an agent of cultural change can be realized only in this way. The word must again and again become flesh.

We can articulate this imperative theologically. God the Father, the power behind the pressure point, gives us our dynamic situation, the breaking down of old "mastered worlds" and the possibilities for new ones. He has put us at a point of pressure that raises the question of life or death for our society and culture. In so doing he comes to us as the destroyer of all our fond idols and comfortable bondages. His power is evident but his goodness is ambiguous, terror and death are mixed with fantastic possibilities.

The Christ-Word, with its grounding in history and in contemporary re-experiences of grace, reveals the deep meaning that lies at the heart of the power of God. The Christ-Word illuminates and communicates the Good News that grace abounds, that the power that confronts us is finally good beyond all that we know. The Christ-Word enables us to live before the reality that is God. God's goodness becomes evident and the meaning of his intentions is unveiled.

So, we have power and its ultimate meaning. There is the experience of God the law and the stroke of liberating grace. Moreover, there is a forward-thrusting movement after the experience of God the law and liberation in the Christ-Event. We have talked about this forward thrust as decisiveness or intentionality. What happens in it is that power and meaning come together in the person or group living out of the Christian story. The gifts and possibilities of the person or group are expressed outward in a thrust into history. The spirit of man with all its possibilities is unleashed with a mighty rush.

The empowering spirit that enhances the possibilities of mystery, depth, and greatness has been referred to in the Christian tradition as the Holy Spirit. It is the Spirit that brings power and meaning together into a new lifestyle that appropriates the gifts of each agent, be it an individual or a group. The third great symbol of the Christian faith, the Holy Spirit, is the empowering thrust in the lifestyle that flows out of the word that allows free life before God. We could diagram this forward thrust with an arrow. The piercing arrow carries the great cry forward into history with focus and intentionality. It moves not out and away from life, but rather right back into and through the pressure point to the new future.

Traditionally, the explication of the doctrine of the Holy Spirit is bound up with the doctrine of the church. This is the case here too, because it is the new corporate lifestyle (church) that is most crucial for our discussion. Only movements or institutions finally have any chance of effecting broad change in a society. They are the generators of widespread social change. Cultural renewal does not just happen spontaneously among individuals; it is carried by social groups. Therefore, we are interested in how the Christian word can take incarnate form in a corporate lifestyle, using the gifts of the secular world that have appeared as impulses toward cultural renewal.

One of the best images of the church in recent years is that of the "social pioneer," suggested and elaborated by H. Richard Niebuhr. Though it was not meant to replace older images, such as the body of Christ or the people of God, it does have evocative power specifically for our discussion of corporate lifestyle. Niebuhr meant his image to imply that the church is a pioneer exploring new vistas in the search for human fulfillment. It is a demonstration project that expresses as many human possibilities as it can. As a pioneering demonstration project, it ought to be out in front of the rest of the society. By striving to approximate the Kingdom of God on earth, it becomes a beacon for the broader society, luring it with persuasive influence to follow suit. It is a sacramental group, a natural human community that is transparent, because of its grounding in the word, to God's presence in human potentiality.

If our analysis of contemporary cultural exhaustion and the frantic search for new lifestyles is at all correct, this image of the social pioneer fits our needs perfectly. It does not lean too heavily on defining the church as an ideological community or as pure outgoing mission or as a bastion of comfort and security. It lies at the juncture of the being and responsibility poles in lifestyle and embraces them both.

The Common Vision

We should be under no illusions about the present state of the church. A vivifying common vision grounded in the word is rare among our congregations. Usually one of two things has happened and both problems stem from the same lack in the church's approach. First, and this is most common, the Christian story has not taken hold in the experience of the people. Many young persons and a surprising amount of older ones fall into this category. God, Jesus Christ, and the Holy Spirit are given proper deference but have no real meaning. Such persons generally go to church for the moral education of their children, for sociability, or simply for the sake of maintaining a life-long habit that makes them "feel right." Another group has appropriated the Christian symbols, but these symbols have been presented to them in such a way that they refer only to experience on the periphery of their lives. They deal only with a certain kind of identification with nature, with mountain-top experiences, with weird happenings, or with death. Experiences of individual and social struggle, of interpersonal interaction, of their own surging possibilities, etc., make no religious sense to these people. God is the God of the gaps, Jesus is a spook, and the Holy Spirit is associated with strange, extrasensory quirks.

In both cases, a woefully inadequate theological training is apparent. The weaknesses of our church should not be attributed to a general lack of seriousness or to moral turpitude. The fact of the matter is that we have done a poor job of communicating the fundamental myths and symbols of the church.

Sometimes they have been taught in a way so literalistic that their appropriation to the experience of the people has been effectively precluded. There is little room for grounding in everyday experience a projection of a God who intervenes like a great puppeteer in the charades of his puppets. And if Jesus is viewed as a disembodied spirit with whom we have daily conversations it is no wonder that the word of Jesus Christ makes little sense. In addition to this wrong-headed and narrow understanding of the symbols of the faith, there is sometimes a woefully inadequate teaching methodology that stands in the way. The nature and function of the symbols and myths may be understood by the clergy, but they are taught in a way so wooden that it practically insures their separation from everyday experience.

We have spent much of our effort in this book trying to explicate the nature and function of the Christian myths and symbols because we are convinced that the renewal of the church as an agent of cultural change must begin at the beginning—the revivification of the common vision of the church. This means a renewed appropriation and communication of the crucial symbols of the faith. Historically speaking, every significant impact upon culture and society has been made by groups that are vitally expressing the common vision they share. That common vision is given shape and content by the central story or myth that defines the group. This was certainly true in the case of the Greeks, with their myth of Prometheus; of the Christians, with their story of Jesus; of the Marxists, with their mythic understanding of alienation and revolution; of the blacks, with their myth of African origins; of the existentialists, with their myth of Sisyphus; and perhaps of the youth, with their story of Aquarius. Many more examples could be given because there have been many significant change-groups in history. All have had myths and symbols that point to and participate in realities that cannot be expressed in other ways because they lie shrouded in the mysterious depths of external reality and human consciousness. The failure of most contemporary utopian communities follows simply from the fact that they have no integrating common vision around which they can establish goals and disciplines. Without such a vision they are ephemeral and doomed to failure.

The interpretation of the Christian symbols of God, Jesus Christ, and the Holy Spirit that has been elaborated in this book constitutes such a common vision. The symbols as they have been interpreted here have great potential for grounding and illuminating the everyday experience of Christian people. They form a perspective on life that aims at a particular lifestyle. This Christian story has a vision about how the cup of being is filled and about how it is emptied. With the use of new cultural impulses the Christian story can indeed incarnate its vision in a concrete lifestyle.

The symbols must first of all be interpreted and appropriated meaningfully in the seminaries of the church. In the past, theology has all too often been taught from a "detached" point of view. Sometimes this was intentional when theology was viewed as a disinterested pursuit of intellectual truth. There is room for this kind of theological approach in the theological schools, indeed it is necessary, but only as "frosting on the cake." For theological speculation makes sense only if the basic appropriation of the Christian symbols has taken place. By appropriation we mean a confrontation by the symbols of the emotions, thoughts, and experiences of the student. The symbols must be presented in a confessional manner and the student must respond with his whole self, not only his intellect. We are not implying here that there must be dogmatic unanimity among either students or faculty. We do mean, however, that both must quit hiding behind "detachment" as a way of dealing with the Christian story.

A second kind of detachment has been unintentional. The symbols were taught as a set of propositions that purportedly grasped the truth of the Christian faith. Besides the arrogance involved in making claims that any human community can capture the truth in its own finite thought-forms, this approach made of Christianity a set of ideological principles that could be confessed without any real grappling with the conditions of sin and grace that far transcend any set of propositions.

In either kind of detachment, seminarians educated under these approaches passed on the sickness to the local congregations. The power of the symbols was lost. Indeed, the very meaning of the symbols was lost for many Christians. In the current crisis of both the church and the society, however, there has been a welcome return in seminary education to the basic appropriation of the Christian symbols. Approaches such as the one in this book have penetrated a good share of seminary students now being trained.

Once the symbols have been appropriated by the clergy and theologically trained laymen of the church, the question becomes one of communication. What teaching methods are effective in enabling people to grasp the significance of the Christian story for their own lives? One group that has been particularly effective in coming up with ways of teaching the Christian faith is the Ecumenical Institute of Chicago. In intensive weekend retreats it has been able to make the faith experientially meaningful to many clergy and lay persons around the country. In their "imaginal" approach to teaching, each concept presented in the course is repeatedly run through the experience of the participants. The approach is highly structured and deductive, sometimes resembling a kind of brainwashing. But it is successful and has contributed a lot to the renewal of a common vision in the church. Because of its tight discipline and deductive approach, however, the Ecumenical Institute teaching programs do come off sometimes in a rigid and ideological way.

Other groups, found mainly in the religious education agencies of the mainline denominations, have tended to take an opposite approach. They have been influenced by nondirective learning approaches and start from the experience of persons and try to work back to the symbols of the Christian faith. This inductive approach takes even more pedagogical skill and theological sophistication than the deductive method. Because of this the denominational programs tend to be hampered by inadequate teaching, which in turn transforms an inductive approach into a mutual sharing of experiences without significant depth interpretation.

In these experiments from both directions, however, more potent pedagogical approaches are being developed. For example, the Lutheran School of Theology at Chicago has developed new programs for teaching entering students and for holding parish renewal retreats that have made use of the contributions of both the deductive and inductive approaches. When an interpretation of the Christian faith such as that given in this book is taught with effective teaching methodologies, it is amazing what can happen in a short time. Congregational groups come alive to the power and meaning of the symbols. They grasp a common vision and move decisively toward renewal of their own life and mission. It raises hopes for a more widespread renewal of religious consciousness in our time.

It is this drive for a common vision, for a new appropriation and communication of the Christian symbols, that is the first priority in developing a corporate lifestyle. All other efforts at church renewal begin at the periphery and will not get at the heart of the matter, which is the revivification of a common religious consciousness flowing out of the Christian word. In terms of lifestyles, it is only a revivification of religious consciousness that can fill the cups of the staggering churches. The milk of the word is needed to fill the cup of each participant in the forging of a new corporate lifestyle.

Covenant Groups

By itself, however, the proclamation and study of the word is not enough to create the new corporate lifestyle. It is an illusion to think that preaching, teaching, and study will lead spontaneously to a Christian community. No matter how vivid the teaching and preaching, sustained human interaction and coordination are tasks that call for an additional strategy. This seems self-evident, but unfortunately most churches never get around to serious community-building. The organizations of a social nature that already exist in local churches sometimes do more to inhibit personal interaction than to promote it. It is tacitly understood that everyone is to be "nice" to each other. Thus, a carefully maintained distance is kept among all members of the group.

In order to overcome the individualism and phony community that we have now, a more human community must be shaped intentionally. The human community that is the church will include *nurture* and *discipline*. By nurture we mean the realization of individual potential within a group context and the enhancing of interpersonal relations. These goals make up the real "care of souls," and both are interdependent: as persons grow within a group the relations between members are enriched and vice versa. This attention to "filling the cups of human beings" can be viewed both as an end in itself and as preparation for the task that lies ahead. It must be cherished as an end in itself because there are persons who must be cared for within the church who will not be able to contribute to the outward-thrusting mission. Those whose cups are constantly being drained of surplus being—the aged, the sick, the emotionally disturbed, etc.— make claim for affirmation and care that is conditionless. They must be attended to whether or not they can participate in the task of mission. For most persons, however, "filling the cups" within a convenant group must be held in tension with "pouring them out" in disciplined mission. Nurture is for the sake of mission.

Discipline is the link between nurture and mission. It enables the creation of a coordinated, strong body for the execution of the task of mission. Nurture and discipline together make up the womb of the church. They gather up the tender seeds that spring up where the word has been sowed, nurture them into strong plants, and discipline them for the struggle that lies ahead.

Discipline is the link between the being and responsibility poles in lifestyle; it is the conjunction between nurture and mission. The word "discipline," however, has a bad reputation in the church. To many it refers to doctrinal stringency or undue attention to minor virtues and vices. But discipline in the authentic sense of the word is indispensible for gathering disparate human energies into coordinated effort. Often, what people want to do conflicts with what they ought to do. Indeed, the notions of what a group ought to do vary extensively. So, in order to discipline unruly wants and various "oughts," a structure of accountability is necessary. Such a structure will enable the group to begin to direct some of its energies outward toward the responsibility pole. An adequate structure of accountability will help the group to maintain a healthy dialectic between the maintenance (nurture) functions of the group and its task (mission) functions. In other words, it will insure a lifestyle that includes the needs of being and the imperatives of responsibility.

Practical methods helpful in forming a structure of accountability are available in the training procedures of institutions specializing in organizational development. Organizational development has brought these different methods of leadership and accountability to explicit consciousness. It has analyzed and charted them in ways that make them available for reduplication. This secular wisdom is another example of how impulses for cultural renewal within the general culture are available for use by the church. But again, like the small group methodology, organizational development is used within the context of meaning and limitation established by the Christian symbols.

The enablement of group accountability is not looked upon merely as a way of increasing the efficiency of a group by doing away with outworn authoritarian structures; it is seen as a means of gathering the gifts and energies of Christians into the interdependent body of Christ. The task of the body is not maximization of profit or better education; it is rather the incarnation and communication of the word of life, the word that enables persons to live their lives and die their deaths. The calling to this task was not issued by an organization embracing a narrow interest; it was issued by the Lord of history himself, who embraces all. Such a task given by such a source must be appropriated with a seriousness that transcends that of secular organizations. Again, a secular gift can be grounded in the Christian religious consciousness.

As the larger congregation spawns smaller units within it that are genuine nurturing and disciplining communities, the lifestyle of individuals and the corporate church itself are changed. Individuals will no longer be satisfied with superficial or dishonest relations outside their groups. They will press for deeper personal relations in all areas of life. Moreover, after experiencing democratic modes of accountability, they will agitate for more democratic modes in other institutions and organizations outside their group. No doubt one of the first structures to be attacked will be the church itself.

Corporately, the lifestyle of the church will begin to take on the shape of the social pioneer. The intimacy and effectiveness of the covenant group, deepened and enriched by the Christian symbols, will give the church a quality of life that is not available in the general society. This quality of life can become a beacon for the rest of society. It can represent the future life of mankind now. Such a style of life will not need to be sold; it will have contagious appeal. When the depth meaning and power of interpersonal life are brought together, the Spirit is vitally present and persuasive.

Mission

Nurture and discipline following from the common vision are not complete in themselves either. The body is born in the word, and grows and is exercised in nurture and discipline. The body must be committed, however. The social pioneer not only develops a rich internal life, it thrusts outward. The two prongs of outward thrust are evangelism and social ministry. These constitute the commitment of the body to action.

By evangelism, we mean active witness to the power and truth of the word. What the word has meant in our past history and in our present lives is to be shared with all. The word must be proclaimed. It must penetrate the population. The body of Christ needs to be replenished by new recruits. Recruitment has always been the sign of a vital social body. Vitality produces an enthusiasm that must be shared.

The other prong of the outward thrust of mission is social ministry. If evangelism is related to liberating grace, then social ministry is related to supportive grace. We cannot control the stroke of liberating grace even though we can proclaim the word. But we can control supportive grace. We can not give persons the power to walk on water, but we can keep them from drowning: we can help ensure their survival amidst the waves and wind of life.

Social ministry itself breaks into two other areas. First, there is social welfare, the works of mercy of the church. This task does not include any direct attempt to change structures by exercising power over against them. It consists, instead, in those efforts to treat the wounds of those harmed by the world. Orphanages, hospitals, homes for the elderly, kindergartens, care for the indigent, sick, and mentally ill, etc., are all modes of mercy. It was fashionable to scorn these ministries during the sixties when structural change was viewed as the only worthwhile target of the church's social efforts. That was both mistaken and arrogant. No matter how good or bad the society, there are always those who need immediate help, who cannot wait for structural change to occur. But the kernel of truth in the attack on the ministry of welfare remains. If the church *only* treats the symptoms of social malfunctions it tacitly opts for the status quo. It must be involved in structural change also. Moreover, if the church does engage in hospital, kindergarten, etc., work, it must be intent on making those ventures authentic demonstration projects that are better than those run by other organizations. If it creates and runs second-rate social agencies, it is wasting its limited money and energies. Welfare projects of great excellence, in contrast, are good lures to the rest of society. Secular agencies will try to approximate the quality of care given in church institutions.

The other area of social ministry can be termed "justing love." It refers to the effort by the corporate church to change the structures of society. The church aims at structural change either indirectly through its laymen in the world or directly through its own use of institutional power. In either case the approach is self-consciously oriented toward structural change. It is shaped by the awareness that in an interdependent world a change in social structures and procedures affects great numbers of persons. Change at the level of public policy gets nearer the roots of social problems than the welfare approach. Thanksgiving baskets to the known poor do not approximate a dignified system of public income maintenance. The former approach is dependent upon sporadic charity; the latter resides in permanent public law.

Local congregations get involved in the quest for justing love when they join a community organization in their neighborhood, when they take a stand on a local issue and work for it, when they join with groups like Operation Bread-basket to promote racial justice, or when they work actively for peace. In these examples, the church as an institution is trying to use its weight to affect political or economic decision-making. In the model of the church that we have been elaborating, each small unit may pick one of the causes as its outlet for public responsibility. On some issues, more coordinated effort may be appropriate. As a social pioneer in lifestyle, the covenant group must include the imperative to exercise social responsibility as well as to create a model community within its own confines.

Of course it is obvious enough that local congregations are not carrying out this forward thrust into the world. Even in the midst of the social action movement of the sixties, too few laymen and too few congregations were significantly involved in evangelism and social ministry. Now, in the burnt-out seventies, the external thrust is almost non-existent.

The reasons for this unhappy situation are manifold. For many the Christian word is not understood as a tremendous summons that impels one into the world. For many, even yet, the Christian faith saves persons from the world, and for them religion has little to do with their own daily life, let alone the problems of society. For others the lack of vitality in communal life within the church creates no overflow of enthusiasm. Their cups are not full enough to share with others either in terms of witness to the word or in terms of social ministry. A much smaller group of persons within the churches has an understanding of the word and has enthusiasm, but lacks know-how or enough comrades of similar persuasion. This group feels frustrated but is constantly on the look-out for opportunities for mission.

The cumulative result of these weaknesses is a floating institution. Institutions, like individuals, can meander through time without focus, skimming over everything with little or no impact. A good number of local congregations have just enough in their cup of being to survive. They do not even float merrily along the stream of history. They have enough to do just to tread water. Other congregations have more buoyance but still live from day to day. They do a little bit of everything—worship, teaching, social missions, care of the sick—so that on paper they appear to have a significant operation going. But their involvement is mere dabbling. They have no real focus and do not plumb the depths of any task or cause. It is probably true, as Stephen Rose has argued in the *Grass Roots Church*, that an adequately functioning church can do *one* thing well. What would it really mean for a local congregation to aim for real excellence in religious education and to focus its skills and energies on that one task?

As we proceed to confront these shortcomings in the external mission of the church, we must be clear about several things. First, there will be no meaningful renewal of social mission without attention to the first two tasks we have already examined, training in the word and nurture/discipline within the church. The enhancement of social ministry can be effective only if it is placed within the context of an overall strategy of renewal. Exhorting a languishing congregation to social ministry as the first step in renewal is a serious error. The summons will not come as part of a whole style of life that follows from the liberating word of God. It will come rather as law and serve only to heighten the guilt and alienation that is already present in the congregation. Idealistic young pastors are prone to this strategic mistake; they fail to place social missions within a comprehensive renewal strategy. Without any base of support behind them, they cut themselves off from the congregation and they themselves become the social mission of the church. Several of the schemes to apply organizational development techniques to congregations in order to aid them in developing social ministry fall prey to the same miscalculation. They assume a grounding in the word and a vital internal life. But that assumption can be seriously mistaken. There may not be enough momentum in the church's life to carry it through such a process.

This is not to argue that there are no individuals in the church who are ready for social mission. There certainly are— the elite five percent! And they should constitute one of the smaller units within the church. Their covenant group can become *the* pioneer in social mission. Even though one part of the body is ready to move, however, other parts are not. It is of utmost importance, therefore, to place social ministry in the context of a comprehensive plan for renewal of corporate lifestyle. For a great number of persons within the local congregation, it may be necessary to start at the being pole, not the responsibility pole of lifestyle.

Earlier, we talked about task-oriented intentionalism as a stance and as a methodology. As a stance, it refers to a posture toward life itself in which individuals or groups decide to enter history, to place their lives significantly within the drama of history. We pointed to the various liberation movements as efforts to summon participants in the movement toward such a stance, to free them from their victim-image and call them to historical significance. For blacks this means freedom from the grinding round of poverty and exclusion that tries to press them to the level of animal life. For women, liberation means freedom from exclusion from the public sphere and the opportunity to pursue careers, public office, and lifestyles of their own choosing. Both movements also try to break with a consumer style of life that in a more sophisticated and seductive way lures people out of the world of public responsibility into the world of sumptuous private living. Intentionalism as a stance calls persons to become the free beings they are. It calls them to exercise their capacity to act into the chain of natural and historical causation, shaping the destiny of themselves and others according to their free determination.

The intentionalist stance, however, is no stranger to the Christian faith. The stroke of liberating grace reunites one with the greatness of his being. He may be alienated from it, but every person has greatness. In the moment of liberation, the person grasps the possibility of living and dying intentionally. He sees that he has been given a life of finite freedom. He realizes that his time and energies are finite, that they are slipping away all the time with every moment and every task. All life is a dying. One need not let his time and energies disperse and float away, however. In his freedom, his greatness, he can decide to use his unique, once-and-for-all gift of life in a focused way. Instead of squandering it on the surface of life, he can decide to plunge to the depths in some task or cause. He need not live and die insignificantly; he can use his life to enter history, to make a splash.

The Christian is clear that his intentional care for the future can be exercised only in a universal context. He is called to live and die on behalf of all. This does not mean that he loves humanity in general and remains detached from concrete causes such as the liberation movements. On the contrary, the Christ-Word insists it is only in the concrete pressure point of present day existence that the Christian forges his ethical life. He must, therefore, plumb the depth of concrete movement. At the same time, however, the consciousness of his responsibility to the whole is never lost. He is clear that the black revolution is finally in behalf of all peoples, and that the women's revolution must be placed in the context of liberation for all, and not just for women. This prophetic consciousness means the difference between a hardened ideological idolization of specific groups and a genuinely humanizing revolution. The universal scope insisted upon by Christian consciousness is an ethical leaven in intentionalist movements of our time.

Once we are clear that an intentional stance in the church is dependent upon its common vision and nurture, we can move to the gifts of intentionalism as a methodology. Intentionalism as a conscious methodology emerged from the natural sciences. The problem-solving method had been codified in that field for decades. Recently, however, the social sciences have systematized problem-solving methods for use in social policy. The potentialities of human planning are now being grasped in fields of human action. Organizational development is a burgeoning field that applies planning methodologies to various endeavors, particularly to business. Organizational development enables agencies systematically to realize their future projects.

The following organizational development methods have already been alluded to earlier but deserve a brief listing here: a conscious, systematic way of establishing contracts between participants in a task; a way of clearly analyzing leadership styles and their consequences; an elaboration of modes of decision-making and their attendant forms of accountability; a series of insights into organizing different interest groups so that each can maintain its interest while contributing to the whole; procedures for building comprehensive models for the future; and a specific set of problem-solving approaches that enable persons to implement the goals they have set themselves.

This systematized, codified wisdom is a great gift to the world. It is shaping the cultural consciousness of persons in many institutions, offering them hope of becoming more intentional in a corporate way. Instead of floating ineffectively, institutions are being given a new ability to decide on priorities and to implement them. Churches, schools, businesses, agencies of all sorts are sending their personnel to laboratories for training in organizational development.

Again, we can only affirm the fantastic gifts these new methods have for enabling the church to realize its mission in the world. Human planning should and is being applied to the future projects of the church. It will enable the churches more effectively to break with floating patterns and to plan for and realize evangelism campaigns, social welfare efforts, and social action projects. Not to use these secular gifts, which are finally gifts of the Lord, is to reject the greatness that human freedom has achieved in managing the future.

But, again, the Christian perspective conditions the use of organizational development in the church and in the world. First, we must be clear that it is essentially a method and cannot insure the intentional *stance* upon which it is dependent for its effective use. Persons must *want* to project their plans into the future. They must believe in the mission they are being called upon to organize. These qualities cannot be produced by a method, but must follow from the common vision and nurture that are prior tasks. In fact, most sophisticated approaches to organizational development are aware that they are dependent upon a prior stance and belief-system. Thus, we cannot idolize organizational development. We know this, that if it is to be intentional, liberation must depend upon the unmanageable grace of God and the free decisiveness of man.

Moreover, as a method, organizational development is morally neutral. It can be used to increase the sale of deodorant, to shoot a rocket to the moon, or to deploy missiles over the face of the earth. Demonic as well as worthy purposes alike can make use of intentionalism as a methodology. In the church, however, it has to be wed to the ethical principle of the church's life and mission. It must enable the church to pour out its being in a more focused way, living on behalf of the humanization of all men.

We can only spell out in a general way the effects of the use of intentionalist methods in helping to realize the mission of the church. The specifics are much too dependent upon local conditions. We would only say that in the process of shaping a corporate intentional lifestyle in the church, the specific gifts of each congregation and smaller units within it would be enabled to enter history in a significant way. Evangelism, social welfare, and social action all demand persons with varied interests and gifts. A sound intentionalism will organize them in such a way that those persons can express the unique gifts they have.

The church has a great opportunity to overcome the floating lifestyles of the surrounding culture. The church need not be a pale reflection of the exhausted patterns around it. If it intentionally rebuilds its corporate lifestyle from the ground up, from the common vision through nurture/discipline to focused mission, it has an opportunity to train the troops who will become the agents of change of the future. Instead of spawning Rieff's "psychological man" or Ferkiss's "bourgeois man," the church can train those who will risk the exposure and vulnerability of decisive action in the world.

Worship and Celebration

In our explication of the corporate lifestyle of the church, we have covered common vision, nurture and discipline, and mission. The word, the community, and the intentional life have been discussed. It would seem that worship and celebration should have been introduced much earlier. And in a chronological sense that is correct. Worship and celebration are activities that ought to go on from the beginning. Without worship, teaching, nurture, and mission would be one dimensional. But we have placed worship and celebration at the end to make a very important point. Meaningful worship can be generated only within the context of the word, of the community, and of an intentional life. Celebration without grounding in a common vision turns into entertainment. Worship without plumbing the depths of interpersonal life is individualistic, not communal. Celebration without engaging in a mission of intentional suffering and death becomes shallow and hypocritical. So, though worship is chronologically simultaneous with the other functions of the church's life, it is also dependent upon them for authenticity.

An excellent description of worship within the Christian community was elaborated by Friedrich Schleiermacher in his reflections on Christian ethics. Worship, he asserted, is the active expression of an internal state of religious self-consciousness. Internal states of feeling are manifested in external expressiveness. Worship has no intent to change the world, only to express in song, music, words, movement, etc., what is internal. Corporate worship is the ascending state of religious self-consciousness within a group. As each individual expresses the religious feeling within him, those who have an abundance contribute to the enhancement of the whole. Those who have less are caught up in the ascending spiral of religious expression. Thus, in authentic worship there is a mutual reinforcement of the religious-self-consciousness of the individual by the whole and of the whole by the individual.

The feeling-states to which Schleiermacher was referring are not arbitrary and subjective. True Christian worship is the expression of feeling-states that correspond to the drama of life as it is interpreted by the Christian story. The symbols of the faith give depth and meaning to the experience of life. It is that depth and meaning that generates the feeling.

Alienation from ourselves, others, and God, for example, leads to feelings of sorrow and remorse. Our constant attempts to escape or float away from the pressure point of God are rehearsed. As we see our lives before God the law our posture is one of repentance. This is the first moment in worship.

We also rehearse the inestimable possibility of life, however. The givenness of creation, of our own lives, of the lives of loved ones, of the opportunities to live fully, etc., are gathered up in feelings of gratitude before the Creator and Sustainer of them all. Especially the gift of the Christ, the word who defines us and enables us to grasp the reality of the grace of God, is met with joy and gladness. Corresponding to this, the moments of grace in our own lives are rehearsed and the appropriate feelings of praise are expressed.

Finally, there is a rehearsal of the moment of decision. The times in everyday life when intentionality was shown, when life was spilled out in a focused way, are brought to consciousness. These are rehearsed, but there are new commitments to the life of mission also. The Holy Spirit who brings power and meaning together in the lives of individuals and groups is invited to carry us forward into the world. The appropriate emotion here is love, but not a sentimental, soft love. It is a firm love that leads to solid promises of commitment to live concretely on behalf of all men. This love is accompanied by a kind of mad joy that dances on the grave of the death that one has decided to die in concrete mission in life.

Thus, repentance, praise, and commitment are the moments of worship. They are accompanied by emotions that express those postures before God. At best, they are expressed within forms that enable *common* worship. Forms are always present. It is merely a matter of which forms are the best channels of expression for the religious feelings grounded in the Christian story.

There is little need to dwell on the problems that inhibit vital worship within our churches. In addition to the lack of common vision, of nurture, and of intentionality, which give worship real substance, there is a cultural drag about which more needs to be said. Whether or not Max Weber's "Protestant ethic" is in fact a real product of Protestant faith, the ethos he described is nevertheless a reality. Our culture, and our churches, are replete with the "Protestant ethos." The sober asceticism that frowns on emotional expression, especially on the part of men, cripples authentic manifestations of religious feeling. The rational control that has been so successful in taming the natural conditions of our existence has also tended to leach out the mystery of the world. "Objective consciousness," dominating rational control built on quantitative methodologies, has disenchanted the world for many people. They cannot break through a one-dimensional apprehension of life. This mind-set obviously makes worship and celebration difficult. This ethos is also imbued with a reluctance to change. Even though there is little vitality in the worship of the church, there is still a fear of something new and different.

The youth culture has been a sharp reaction to precisely the ethos delineated above. If anything, that culture has been expressive. The inhibitions against emotionality have been thrown off. Joy, sorrow, anger, etc., flow easily among the young. Their language is laced with highly charged words that were once considered unfit for public use. This renewed expressiveness has meant a lot for local churches. It is a rare church that has not experienced in some way or another a folk song or rock setting of the liturgy. There is little doubt that these new forms have more possibility for expression, at least for younger persons, than the older forms.

The youth culture has tended to reject a dominating, aggressive stance toward life. Competition and success are bad words. Young persons are aiming for a more symbiotic relation with the world. They are learning simply to *be*, to coexist gently with all that is about them. But this coexistence does not lead to a stale internal life. On the contrary, the inner consciousness is extremely active, sometimes even violent, if rock music can be taken as an authentic expression of youth consciousness. These twin gifts, the ability simply to *be* and the capacity to express in all kinds of forms the reflections on simply being, are gifts to our society and our churches. An activistic ethos has difficulty worshiping and celebrating. The youth are teaching us to take our time, to be, to enjoy, and to express the feelins that follow.

Finally, the youth culture has been much more sensitive to the mystery of life than the older generations. This follows naturally from the first two points above. Its appreciation for the nonrational leads it to all sorts of weird aberrations, but it also gives the youth culture an openness to religious consciousness that was not present in a corporate way in the generation of their fathers and mothers. For example, the climate for religious renewal on the campuses is more friendly now than it has been for some time.

The church can honestly applaud much of what is happening among the youth. Their reactions on the whole have been appropriate and helpful in building a more human culture. The youth culture has given much to society and to the church. But like the small group movement and task-oriented intentionalism, the gifts of the youth culture are not used blindly by a church that is adequately grounded in its own story and symbols.

The most important thing the church can bestow upon the impulses of the youth culture is an objective grounding. The youth culture is so volatile and experimental that it falls prey to every sort of faddism. If its gifts are to be used by the church, they must be grounded in the Christian symbols of God, Jesus Christ, and the Holy Spirit. Expressions of gratefulness float around in confusion unless there is a referrent for the gratitude. Sorrow, protest, commitment, love are only sporadic emotions if they are not placed within a broader, and finally universal, context of meaning. The youth search for these contexts of meaning but tend to come away from their pursuits with ephemeral solutions.

Objective grounding in the Christian story also provides an anchor in the historical past that mitigates the implicit and sometimes explicit contempt for the past shown by the youth culture. Some of the contempt is understandable because the Christian past has been presented to them in a deadly and authoritarian way. Under such conditions they cannot feel part of the long story that extends from the very beginning to the very end. But a Christian stance cannot toss off its grounding in history. The word has come down through history and has been communicated in worship, song, and customs that must, even when they seem out of vogue, be treated with respect. Respect for the past need not curtail experimentation. It only gives experimentation a better grounding and forestalls rampant subjectivity.

Though the church can appreciate the youth culture's exploration of the being pole of life, it must demur from a premature expectation of the age of Aquarius. The gift for just being and not doing is an important one for a restive American culture. But an adequate Christian lifestyle is more balanced. There is too much to be done in the world. The responsibility pole of lifestyle must be embraced. Moreover, the faith is clear that lasting joy and peace come only in relation to disciplined suffering and dying in concrete mission.

The cultural impulses of the youth movement offer much to both church and society. In the church the gifts of expression and sensitivity to mystery are placed within the context of its whole life. In such a role these gifts will aid in revitalizing the worship and celebration of the church.

As we close our discussion of corporate lifestyle, we would like to make two remarks. First, the four elements of church life—common vision, nurture/discipline, mission, and worship—provide a comprehensive framework for the renewal of the church. A corporate lifestyle in the church that has the power to bridge the gap between Christian consciousness and secular society cannot be built quickly or haphazardly. The renewal of a local congregation's life is a long-term process that never ends. Real results should be expected only after years of work. Renewal is not only a long process, it is also one that demands strategy. All the gifts of organizational development must be used to sharpen the intentionality of renewal-oriented churches. There must be an overall plan for renewal.

Second, the preceding elaboration of steps toward a new corporate lifestyle is not just wild speculation. There are specific local congregations that are living in the future now. The Holy Spirit has been working. In fact, the strategy elaborated here has been stimulated by participation in and observation of those congregations. There are real possibilities for creating new corporate lifestyles in local congregations. The time is ripe. Also, there are imaginative experiments in the seminaries of the church that have attempted to create models of corporate lifestyle that may later be useful in building strategies of renewal in local congregations. The resources of seminaries enable them to experiment with new forms of corporate lifestyle. This experimentation is going on now and will no doubt emerge more frequently in local congregations as time goes on.

We have a remaining task. We must probe the relation of this developing corporate lifestyle to the crisis of our technological society. What will it mean in relation to our economic, social, political, and cultural problems?

The cultural impulses themselves will have an impact on society apart from whatever use the church may make of them. The youth culture will continue to add color and experimental verve to the broader culture. With its animosity toward the rational mind-set of domination and its interest in being rather than doing, it will tend to dampen the economic and political activism of past American culture. Its neo-naturalism, moreover, bodes well for a more sensitive ecological consciousness. The small group movement will continue to offer the possibility of growth in human potential and intimacy in a mobile, rootless society. This will mean a lot for the middle classes in particular. Finally, task-oriented intentionalism will continue to call minority groups into history that have been thus far locked out. We can expect the various liberation movements to lose their harsh rhetoric and utopian schemes as they enter into the historical process. An appreciation of the various shades of gray in the real historical world tends to bring new participants in it down to earth rather rapidly. Intentional methodologies will enable private and public agencies to project and implement their plans more effectively, and as these methodologies reach into institutions that have tendencies to drift—the church, the school, government agencies—new possibilities for more focused action will come their way.

At this time, however, these cultural impulses are going in different directions. The youth are mistrustful of both the small group movement and intentionalism as new forms of manipulation and "repression." The small group movement shies away from the ambiguous and unruly public world where intentionalism is most at home, and the intentionalists look upon the youth culture as ineffectual and the small group movement as "navel-gazing."

These impulses toward cultural renewal invite a coordinated and centered use. The church has the vision and the symbology that can pull them together into a corporate lifestyle that not only makes good use of the gifts of such impulses but also gives them an added dimension of depth and meaning. The significance of all three is enhanced when illuminated by Christian symbols.

When the impulses toward cultural renewal are gathered up into the church's corporate lifestyle, a potent instrument of the Spirit will be created. Although overstatement and unrealism are a temptation, we would venture the following reflections about the future impact of the new corporate lifestyle that is emerging in the church.

The greatest and most significant impact of the church's corporate lifestyle will be directed to the cultural level. The church has little chance of changing economic, social, and political realities in a direct way. It has too little power for that. Its impact will be much more on the lifestyle of the American people. The underlying cultural substratum—values, perspectives, customs, sensitivities—is where the church is most at home as an agent of change. This has been true historically and will continue to be true in the future.

As an agent of change, the church will be acting in a milieu of cultural exhaustion. The lifestyle of psychological man, though popular as a cultural ideal, will not be able to meet the needs of being or the imperatives of responsibility. The sensate character of our consumption-oriented society insures only continued floating and senseless motion.

It is here that the word of life has its greatest social significance. The basic problem of man is within him. Does he, in the midst of the pressures of life, choose defiance of or escape from the holy power? If he chooses either, he adopts a lifestyle of defense and evasion. If he opens himself up to the grace that transforms him, on the other hand, he adopts a lifestyle of openness and decisiveness. The Christian word calls all mankind to the latter. It invites persons to walk on life and to die their deaths on behalf of all. And when the word takes hold, a real revolution of the heart takes place. The foundations are shifted and persons are able to live with vigor and intentionality. This means the difference between a moribund and a vital culture.

Anchored in this word, the corporate lifestyle of the church will make greater inroads into America's middle classes. There is where the church is and there is where it is most important that changes in lifestyle be effected.

As more Christians abandon the consumption lifestyle for the sake of a more human alternative, they will be less apt to use their economic role for an ever-increasing standard of living. It may become more possible to shunt more of our wealth and energy into the public realm where it can be put to use in opening doors for the other America that churns so restlessly in the bowels of our society. Moreover, a population whose lifestyle demands concern for a mysterious universe of being, may be able to temper its lifestyle more in accordance with its real needs than with its limitless wants. It may coexist more harmoniously with the natural world and with the rest of the human world.

The rootlessness and unwanted anonymity of American society can find a needed response in the corporate lifestyle of the church. As the church develops nurture and discipline within intimate small groups, real alternatives to our atomized society will become available, and persons will not have to be cajoled into the church. The quality of its life will be self-evident.

The isolation from political power in American society is just as much a matter of lifestyle as it is of "repression" by the "establishment." Too much of our population has been persuaded that a floating consumer life is the good life. But such a misconception cannot last. Human life has a greatness that calls out to be unleashed in significant action. The corporate lifestyle of the church nurtures such greatness. Each man living out of the word has the freedom to thrust his life effectively into the stream of history. The intentionality that follows from this not only leads to responsible action on behalf of the world; it also fills the cup of being. Free action in the public sphere puts man in touch with the greatness of his being.

Thus, the church will have its most direct impact on the culture of the people. This cultural impact will have economic, social, and political implications. Moreover, while it is working on this cultural level, the church cannot neglect the direct impact it can have in politics, economics, and society. As a social pioneer, the church not only strives after new demonstration projects; it acts more directly in the world also. The cultural imperative must not become a substitute for the political imperative.

The ancient injunction of the Christian Gospel is to penetrate all of life with the ethos of radical trust in God and radical love for the brethren. The imperative was heard and acted upon. The Middle Ages represent such a struggle for interpenetration of word and world. But that old world is gone. Vestiges of it cling to existence even now but we know they are doomed. The church can no longer run the world. The new world is aborning and the church has a new role—it must carry off its revolution without pomp and political power. The world must be persuaded by the church, not ruled by it.

The goal of this revolution by cultural persuasion is that more and more of life becomes transparent to the presence of the Lord. And as the divine presence becomes more powerfully present, the hallowing of life proceeds. As every facet of life expresses the holy power that sustains it, human realization becomes a reality. When God is all in all, man will be complete.

Christians have always been called to an errand in the wilderness. At their best they are a tent people, midway between the no longer and the not yet. The errand is to press forward the impulses toward humanization that have been in process since time began. The relentless Power pushes from the past and the beckoning Promise pulls from the future, and the word explodes with possibilities in the present.

BIBLIOGRAPHICAL ESSAY

BIBLIOGRAPHICAL ESSAY

Footnotes and other kinds of references have consciously been eliminated from the text of *Wandering in the Wilderness*. The following brief list of titles, however, indicates the chief sources used by the author.

The Signs of the Times
1. Comprehensive studies:
    Arendt, Hannah. *The Human Condition.* New York: Doubleday Anchor Books, 1958.
    Ellul, Jacques. *The Technological Society.* New York: Knopf, 1964.
    Ferkiss, Victor. *Technological Man.* New York: Braziller, 1969.
2. Problems of economics:
    Banfield, Edward. *The Unheavenly City.* Boston: Little, Brown, 1970.
    Galbraith, John Kenneth. *The Affluent Society.* Boston: Houghton Mifflin, 1958.
    _____. *The New Industrial State.* Boston: Houghton Mifflin, 1967.
    Harrington, Michael. *The Other America.* Baltimore: Penguin Books, 1963.
3. Problems of culture:
    Dawson, Christopher. *Religion and Culture.* New York: Sheed and Ward, 1948.

Rieff, Philip. *The Triumph of the Therapeutic.* New York: Harper and Row, 1966.

Troeltsch, Ernst. *The Social Teachings of the Christian Church,* 2 Vols. New York: Harper and Row, 1960.

van Leeuwen, Arend. *Christianity in World History.* New York: Scribner's, 1966.

Viereck, Peter. "The Revolution of the Heart," *Ramparts,* August, 1966.

Weber, Max. *The Protestant Ethic and the Spirit of Capitalism.* New York: Scribner's, 1958.

Sources of Renewal

1. Youth Culture:

Earisman, Del. *How Now Is the Now Generation?* Philadelphia: Fortress, 1971.

Reich, Charles. *The Greening of America.* New York: Random House, 1970.

Roszak, Theodore. *The Making of a Counter Culture.* New York: Doubleday Anchor Books, 1969.

Saffen, Wayne. *Youth Today.* Philadelphia: Fortress, 1971.

2. The small group movement:

Bradford, Leland; Gibb, Jack; and Benne, Kenneth (eds.). *T-Group Theory and Laboratory Method.* New York: Wiley, 1964.

Harris, Thomas. *I'm OK — You're OK.* New York: Harper and Row, 1969.

Luft, Joseph. *Group Processes: An Introduction to Group Dynamics.* Palo Alto: The National Press, 1963.

Schutz, William. *Joy: Expanding Human Awareness.* New York: Grove, 1967.

3. Intentionalism:

Bennis, Warren; Benne, Kenneth; and Chin, Robert. *The Planning of Change.* New York: Holt, Rinehart and Winston, 1969.

——————. *Organizational Development.* New York: Addison Wesley Series, 1965.

Blake, Robert and Morton, Jane. *The Managerial Grid.* Houston: Gulf Publishing Co., 1964.

God's Pressure Point

Niebuhr, H. Richard. *Radical Monotheism and Western Culture.* New York: Harper and Row, 1960.

——————. *The Responsible Self.* New York: Harper and Row, 1963.

Niebuhr, Reinhold. *The Nature and Destiny of Man.* New York: Scribner's, 1943.

Tillich, Paul. *Systematic Theology,* Vol. 1. Chicago: University of Chicago Press, 1951.

——————. *Dynamics of Faith.* New York: Harper and Row, 1957.

The Church and the Liberating Word

Niebuhr, H. Richard. *The Meaning of Revelation.* New York: Macmillan, 1941.

Tillich, Paul. *The New Being.* New York: Scribner's, 1955.

Toward a Renewed Lifestyle

Tillich, Paul. *Systematic Theology,* Vol. 3. Chicago: University of Chicago Press, 1963.